VOLUME SIX Leader Guide

Everything You Need to Know to Be a

A year of Bible study for 6th graders

VICKIE KNIERIM
Editor
ANDREA HULTMAN
Production Specialist
MIKE LANG
Graphic Designer
BETTY KAY WASSERMAN
Technical Specialist
JUDY LATHAM
Manager, Children's VBS-
Ventures Section
DAVID MORROW
Director, Children's Sunday
School Ministry Department
LOUIS B. HANKS
Associate Division Director,
Sunday School Group
BILL L. TAYLOR
Director, Sunday School Group

KEN PARKER
G. G. MATHIS
RHONDA VANCLEAVE
Writers

Send questions/comments to:
Judy Latham, 127 Ninth Avenue,
North, Nashville, TN 37234-0178
or EMAIL jlatham@lifeway.com.

*Everything You Need to Know
to Be a Teenager—Leader Guide*
(ISBN 0-7673-9476-3) is pub-
lished by LifeWay Christian
Resources of the Southern
Baptist Convention, 127 Ninth
Avenue, North, Nashville, TN
37234-0113: James T. Draper,
Jr., President, LifeWay Christian
Resources of the Southern
Baptist Convention; Ted Warren,
Executive Vice President,
LifeWay Christian Resources;
Gene Mims, President, LifeWay
Church Resources, a division of
LifeWay Christian Resources.

If you need help with an order
WRITE Customer Service
Center, 127 Ninth Avenue North,
Nashville, TN 37234-0113; FAX
(615) 251-5933; EMAIL
CustomerService@lifeway.com;
or PHONE 1-800-458-2772. Mail
address changes to: Everything
You Need to Know to Be a
Teenager, 127 Ninth Avenue,
North, Nashville, TN 37234-0113.

Unless otherwise noted, all
Scripture printed herein is from
the Holy Bible, *New International
Version.* Copyright 1973, 1978,
1984 by International Bible
Society. Used by permission.

We believe the Bible has God
for its author; salvation for its
end; and truth, without any mix-
ture of error, for its matter. The
1998 statement of *The Baptist
Faith and Message* is our
doctrinal guideline.

EVERYTHING

Everything a Leader Needs to Know about

You have entered a new dimension! Teaching sixth graders is a world apart from teaching children and youth—you know it and we know it! That's why we have created a second set of *Everything You Need to Know to Be a Teenager.*

Preteens need to discover what the Bible says, demonstrate their understanding of what they learn, and be discipled in their relationship with Christ. You need something different to help you teach these kids in Sunday School, on retreats, or in Wednesday night Bible study—here it is!

Everything You Need to Know to Be a Teenager is a twelve-month Bible study in four volumes. Each volume contains a series of twelve Bible studies based on Christian doctrine, Christian life choices, and Christian character traits. In addition, a bonus session is offered in each volume for use on special occasions like Christmas and Easter or for special studies on Christian citizenship or the ordinances of baptism and the Lord's Supper.

Each unit of *Everything You Need to Know to Be a Teenager* has a **Unit Direction** that describes the topic to be studied, learned, and applied. The topics cover things preteens are interested in and subjects preteens need to learn about as they prepare for their teenage years.

Each session contains a **Life Destination** that helps you know what you are going to accomplish and what preteens will learn.

The Bible study schedule contains these elements:

DISCUSS AND DO

contains interactive methods designed to focus the attention of preteens and spark interest in the Bible study. These activities help sixth graders connect real-life situations and needs with the biblical content to be studied. Preteens may participate in games, watch a video, conduct experiments, discuss questions, or research current events.

DIG gets sixth graders into the Bible study. Preteens search Bible passages to discover biblical principles on which to base life decisions. Sixth graders may study Bible word meanings, compare Bible translations, paraphrase Bible stories, or complete verse-by-verse studies of specific Bible passages.

DECIDE gives sixth graders the opportunity to practice the biblical principles they learn in a safe, non-threatening atmosphere. Sixth graders might respond to case studies, participate in role-plays, write personal commitments, or suggest ways of dealing with real-life situations.

EVERYTHING

Everything You Need to Know to Be a Teenager

Everything You Need to Know to Be a Teenager offers the following resources to get preteens into learning:

The *Leader Guide* contains teaching plans for twelve regular Bible study sessions and one special study session. Each session provides a Bible study for leaders and hints to help you make the most of your teaching opportunity. The guide also includes a reproducible page for each unit of study. A fellowship idea is provided in each guide to help you plan a fun outreach fellowship to reinforce the biblical principles studied in each volume.

The *Preteen Handbook* contains thirteen pages for preteens to use during the Bible study sessions—one page per session. These pages provide a variety of activities designed to reinforce biblical learning. Preteens will record responses, complete puzzles, draw pictures, answer questions, match facts, and study definitions in "Factionary." Pages are perforated for easy removal for distribution. A "How to Become a Christian" page is also included in the *Preteen Handbook*.

Six posters are included in each volume of *Everything You Need to Know to Be a Teenager* to spark interest and provide support for the Bible study session. Unit themes, games, and other activities are printed on the four-color posters.

Three great gadgets are provided in each volume for leaders and preteens to use to play games, demonstrate ideas, and respond to life situations.

A **video** containing six segments is included in each volume. Each video segment relates to a specific session and is designed to prompt discussion and reinforce learning.

Each volume of *Everything You Need to Know to Be a Teenager* is packaged in one box containing all the resources listed above for three months of great Bible study. You may order extra *Leader Guides* and *Preteen Handbooks*. (Each leader will need a guide, and each preteen will need a handbook).
    Everything You Need to Know to Be a Teenager remembers that preteens (and their leaders) like to have fun while learning. Your sixth graders are going to love learning biblical truths from *Everything You Need to Know to Be a Teenager!*

Celebrate! Romans 6:23

Use this fellowship to celebrate God's gift of salvation through His Son, Jesus. Devotional topics that reinforce the biblical principles covered in this volume might include Jesus' birth, salvation, ministry, kindness, and relationships with family and friends. Refer to the "Bible Study for Leaders" in each session for additional devotional ideas.

Invitations: Create invitations by pulling five-inch pieces of ribbon though holes punched in colored three-by-five-inch cards. Tie the ribbon in a bow, write fellowship information on the card, and place in an envelope with some paper confetti.

Decorations: Decorate the room with lots of streamers, balloons, and paper confetti. Provide party hats and noisemakers. Wrap empty boxes with colorful paper and bows. Set boxes in various places around the room.

Games:

• **What's Inside?**—Wrap five inexpensive gifts in boxes of various sizes and shapes. Disguise the gifts by adding weight, special padding, a jar of pebbles, etc. Number each gift and display it on a table at the front of the room. Make a master list of ten possible things that might be in the gifts (five correct, five incorrect), and attach it to the wall above the gift table. Wrap an empty shoe box, minus the lid, in wrapping paper. Provide pencils and writing paper. Allow preteens to pick up and shake the gifts to determine "what's inside." Instruct preteens to number a piece of paper 1-5 and write in their guesses. Tell preteens to fold their papers, write their names on the outside, and place the papers in the box provided. Allow preteens to visit the gift table to make their guesses throughout the celebration. When all preteens have had the opportunity to guess what's inside, unwrap each gift. Give a small prize to each person who guessed correctly.

• **Wrap it Up!**—Determine the gift wrapping champions by challenging pairs of preteens to wrap a gift with one person using only her right hand while her partner uses only her left hand. Provide empty boxes, wrapping paper, scissors, tape, and ribbon for each pair. Say "go" and watch the fun begin. The first team to complete the task wins.

• **Package Parade**—Form teams of four to five preteens. Direct each team to choose someone from their team to represent them in a package parade. Tell preteens that they will have ten minutes to "wrap" their package. Provide rolls of toilet paper or paper towels, newspapers, ribbon, yarn, scissors, and tape. Enlist several adult leaders to serve as judges. When the "packages" have been "wrapped," instruct all entries to walk or wobble across the front of the room for judging. The best looking "package" wins.

Food: Make a giant cake by placing several 9-by-12-inch cakes side-by-side and icing them together. Use decorator icing to write "Celebrate!" across the top of the cake. Sprinkle with candy confetti. For fun, use a different kind of cake mix for each 9-by-12-inch section. It will be a surprise to discover what's inside.

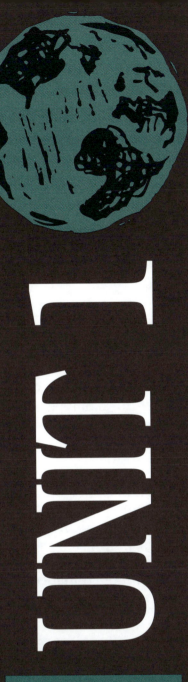

He Did That for Me?

Session 1: Me? A Sinner?

Focal Passages: Romans 3:9-26; 1 John 1:8-10
Life Destination: Preteens will realize their need for redemption as they examine the sin in the world and acknowledge the sin in their own lives.
Memory Verse: For all have sinned and fall short of the glory of God, and are justified freely by his grace through the redemption that came by Christ Jesus. *Romans 3:23-24*

Session 2: He Died for Me?

Focal Passages: Romans 6:23; Romans 5:8; Acts 3:19; Ephesians 2:8-9; Romans 10:9-10,13
Life Destination: Preteens will understand that salvation is available to them only through personal faith in Christ as they repent of their sin, seek His forgiveness, and make Him the Lord of their lives.
Memory Verse: For the wages of sin is death, but the gift of God is eternal life in Christ Jesus our Lord. *Romans 6:23*

Session 3: I Can Be Victorious!

Focal Passages: Romans 7:18–8:2; 1 Corinthians 15:57-58
Life Destination: Preteens will understand the reality of the Christian's continuing struggle with sin and recognize that Jesus is their ally in this struggle.
Memory Verse: Therefore, there is now no condemnation for those who are in Christ Jesus. *Romans 8:1*

Session 4: A Brand New Me

Focal Passage: Romans 12:1-21
Life Destination: Preteens will understand the difference that Christ's transforming power can make in a Christian's life and will discover how they can experience that power in their own lives.
Memory Verse: Therefore, I urge you, brothers, in view of God's mercy, to offer your bodies as living sacrifices, holy and pleasing to God—this is your spiritual act of worship. *Romans 12:1*

Unit Direction

In this unit, preteens will discover that:
• Everyone has sinned and needs redemption.
• Christ died for our sins.
• We can have eternal life through Christ.
• We can be victorious in our ongoing battle with sin.
• We can have new life through Christ's transforming power.

Session 1
Me? A Sinner?

FOCAL PASSAGES:
Romans 3:9-26; 1 John 8-10

MEMORY VERSE:
For all have sinned and fall short of the glory of God, and are justified freely by his grace through the redemption that came by Christ Jesus.
Romans 3:23-24

LIFE DESTINATION:
Preteens will realize their need for redemption as they examine the sin in the world and acknowledge the sin in their own lives.

How This Session Relates to Salvation

Before a person can be saved, he must first realize that he is lost. This is true for children, youth, and adults. In this unit of study, preteens will come to understand their need for redemtption as they discover what it means to be a sinner.

Bible Study for Leaders

The apostle Paul wrote his letter to the Christians in Rome because of his concern about a disease that affects every person. The disease is sin. Its consequences are more serious than any physical illness.

Our Spiritual Illness

In the first three chapters of Romans, Paul made it clear that this spiritual illness affects everyone. God's chosen people, the Jews, thought the answer to the sin problem was found in keeping the laws that God had given to Moses. However, Paul pointed out in the second chapter of Romans, that no Jew had ever been able to keep the law. The Jews were just as guilty before God as the non-Jews (Gentiles). Both "Jews and Gentiles alike are all under sin" (Rom. 3:9).

Paul followed a common Jewish teaching method of quoting Old Testament passages, such as Psalm 14:1-3, to support his claim. He concluded that "the whole world" is "held accountable to God" (Rom. 3:19). In the judgment court of God we all stand condemned with no excuse, no defense. As Paul said so clearly in Romans 3:23, we "all have sinned and fall short of the glory of God."

God's Solution for Our Situation

So what hope do we have? What is the solution to the sickness of sin? In Romans 3:21-22 Paul explained that God has provided a new way of having our guilt removed, a way that does not depend on our ability to keep all of God's laws. The new way, Paul said, "comes through faith in Jesus Christ" (Rom. 3:22). God's holiness demands payment—a sacrifice—to remove the guilt of sin. In His mercy and grace God Himself provided the sacrifice in the form of His only Son Jesus Christ. In this way God maintained justice (Rom. 3:25-26) while providing a solution to the sickness of sin.

What We Must Do

Since we are all guilty before God and deserve His wrath (Rom. 1:18), what must we do to avoid His judgment? The first step is found in the first letter of John the apostle. We must begin by admitting our guilt and throwing ourselves on the mercy of God. If we refuse to admit our guilt, John said that "we deceive ourselves" (1 John 1:8). Admitting our guilt and acknowledging our mistakes is not an easy thing to do. But if we refuse, we are only hurting ourselves and, in addition, calling God a liar (1 John 1:10). Once we do confess our sinful nature, God will be faithful to His promise to "forgive us our sins and purify us from all unrighteousness" (1 John 1:9).

DISCUSS AND DO

GET READY

• Gather: *Preteen Handbooks*, current newspapers and news magazines, two large sheets of paper, a felt-tip marker, masking tape, pencils, enough half sheets of paper for each student present to have one, a shoe box.

• Get this item from the resource box: checkered flag.

GET SET

• Arrange chairs in circles with five to six chairs in each circle. Place several newspapers and magazines in the center of each circle.

• Attach two large sheets of paper to a focal wall.

GET STARTED

1. Discover evidence of sin. As preteens arrive, direct them to one of the circles of chairs. Instruct preteens to tear articles and ads out of the newspapers and magazines provided that show evidence of sin in today's world.

After about five minutes, wave the checkered flag and call for each group to explain how its collection of ads and articles reflects the sin in the world.

2. Identify sins. Give each preteen a half sheet of paper and a pencil. Instruct students to make a list of sins that tempt preteens. When preteens have completed their assignment, direct them to fold their papers in half and place them in the shoe box as you pass it around the room.

After collecting the lists, call for two volunteers to take turns taking a list from the box and reading it aloud. Enlist an adult leader to write responses on one of the large sheets of paper posted on the focal wall. (Place checkmarks by the sins that are mentioned more than once.)

Invite volunteers to suggest a definition of sin. Write responses on the second large sheet of paper posted on the wall.

Call for a volunteer to read aloud the definition of sin from "Factionary" on page 7 of the *Preteen Handbook.* Explain that sin is basically a decision to go against God.

DIG

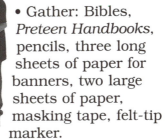

GET READY

• Gather: Bibles, *Preteen Handbooks*, pencils, three long sheets of paper for banners, two large sheets of paper, masking tape, felt-tip marker.

• Get this item from the resource box: key.

• Prepare banners by using a felt-tip marker to write "Hard to Break" on one of the long sheets of paper and "Guilty" on another. Leave the remaining banner blank.

• Make a copy of the "Get into Heaven" ticket found on page 24 (Stuff to Copy) for each preteen present.

GET STARTED

3. Determine what it means to be "under sin." Write the letters "DUI" on a large sheet of paper. Invite a volunteer to explain their

STEP

1

HINT

Scan the magazines and newspapers you gather before the session to make sure there are no offensive ads or photos that might distract preteens from their task. Tear out any objectionable material before the session.

STEP 3

HINT

Be sensitive as you lead in the discussion of bad habits. Do not allow preteens to criticize or make fun of others who may have difficulty with certain habits.

Emphasize that while some habits may be worse than others, all sin is equal in God's eyes.

STEP 5

HINT

Cut copies of today's memory verse (Romans 3:23-24) from page 33 of the *Preteen Handbook*. Distribute the cards to preteens as they examine Romans 3:21-26. Encourage preteens to mark their Bibles with the cards to remind them of their sin problem and their opportunity to accept God's gift of salvation.

meaning. *("DUI" or "Driving Under the Influence" refers to driving a vehicle while under the influence of alcohol or drugs.)* Tell preteens that Paul said we are all under the influence of something. Direct preteens to read Romans 3:9 and the corresponding information in "Factionary" on page 7 of the *Preteen Handbook* to discover what Paul meant. *(We are all under the influence of sin.)*

Call for volunteers to name some bad habits that preteens might have. *(Smoking, cursing, gossiping, eating junk food.)* Explain that the habit of sin is hard to break. Attach the "Hard to Break" banner to a focal wall.

Ask: "What does the jury foreman in a court of law say when the jury is convinced the defendant has broken the law?" *(We find the defendant guilty.)* Attach the "Guilty" banner to the focal wall. Tell preteens that both banners reflect what Paul meant by being "under sin."

4. Compare Scriptures.

Form teams of four to six persons. Direct preteens to turn to "Check it Out!" on page 8 of the *Preteen Handbook*. Instruct teams to match the verses in Psalms with the passages from Romans 3:10-18. When teams have completed their assignment, read aloud each passage from Psalms and call for volunteers to read the corresponding passage from Romans. *(Answers: Ps. 5:9—Rom. 3:13a; Ps. 10:7—Rom. 3:14; Ps. 14:1-3—Rom. 3:10-11; Ps. 36:1—Rom. 3:18; Ps. 40:3—Rom. 3:13b.)* Explain that Jewish rabbis

often quoted from the Old Testament to support their teachings and that Paul used that same method.

Review the main truths Paul was trying to teach in Romans 3:10-18. *(All have sinned–Rom. 3:10-13; Sin can show itself in awful ways–Rom. 3:14-17; The habit of sin can cause a person to forget to respect God–Rom. 3:18.)*

5. Describe our situation because of sin.

Say: "If you were to ask the students at your school what it takes for a person to get to heaven, what would they say?" List responses on a large sheet of paper. Review responses and circle any items that relate to doing good deeds.

Explain that there were people in Paul's day that thought that doing good deeds was enough to get you into heaven. Guide preteens to see how Paul responded to this concept by asking them to read silently Romans 3:19-20 and the corresponding entries in "Factionary" on page 7 of the *Preteen Handbook*. Call for for a volunteer to identify Paul's response. *("No one will be declared righteous in his sight by observing the law"–v. 20).* Continue by determining what Paul said about the purpose of the law *("through the law we became conscious of sin"–v. 20).*

Instruct preteens to read silently Romans 3:21-26 and complete "Who Is It?" on page 8 of the *Preteen Handbook* to determine why Paul said that we can't depend on good deeds to get us into heaven. After a few minutes, call for volunteers

to share the answers.
(Answers: 1. God or Jesus;
2. everyone; 3. everyone;
4. everyone; 5. Jesus; 6. God.)
Ask: "Why did Paul say good
deeds were not enough?"
(Because all have sinned—
v. 23—and therefore all stand
guilty before God.)

**6. Complete a "Get into
Heaven" ticket.** Emphasize
that we need help to overcome our sin problem. Hold
up the key. Call for volunteers to describe the func-
tions of a key. (Keys allow us
to enter or leave a place that
is secured by a lock.) Say:
"Being under sin is like being
locked in chains. We cannot
free ourselves."

Direct preteens to complete
"Key Word Focus" on page 7
of the Preteen Handbook to
discover God's answer (His
key) to the problem of sin.
After a few minutes, call for
responses. (Answers: all, fall,
justified, grace, redemption,
Christ Jesus.)

Distribute to each student
a "Get into Heaven" ticket.
Instruct preteens to complete
each section of the ticket in
light of Romans 3. When preteens have completed the
assignment, call for volunteers to share their responses. Use the "Bible Study for
Leaders" to clarify responses.

7. Create a banner. Ask:
"Why is it so difficult to admit
that we are sinners?"
(Possible responses: shame,
embarrassment, sadness.)
Invite preteens to follow along
in their Bibles as you read
aloud 1 John 1:8-10. Ask:
"What are the consequences
of refusing to admit our sin?"
(We deceive ourselves;

the truth is not in us; we call
God a liar; God's Word has no
place in our lives.) "What are
the results of admitting our
guilt?" (God will forgive our
sins and purify us from all
unrighteousness.)

Encourage students to
suggest ideas for a banner
that illustrates what happens
when we confess our sin.
Lead preteens to determine
the best idea and write it the
remaining long sheet of
paper. Attach this banner to
the focal wall near the "Hard
to Break" and the "Guilty"
banners.

DECIDE
GET READY
• Get this item
from the resource
box: foam hand.

GET STARTED
**8. Determine
where you stand.**
Use the foam hand
to call attention to the three
banners you have posted to
the focal wall. Say: "We can
all stand under the first two
banners because we are all
guilty and we all have trouble
breaking the sin habit. But,
not everyone can stand
under the third banner. Only
those who have confessed
their sin to God can receive
His forgiveness."

Lead preteens to bow their
heads and close their eyes for
a few minutes of silent prayer
as they consider where they
stand. Invite any preteen who
would like to learn more
about what it means to confess their sins to God to talk
with an adult leader. Close
with prayer thanking God for
His love and forgiveness.

STEP
6

HINT

Possible answers for the
"Get into Heaven" ticket
might include: Admit: all
who believe; Payment: death
of Jesus; Cost: free to
those who believe in Jesus;
Benefits: freed from guilt
and power of sin; Good
until: forever.

STEP
8

HINT

Some preteens may not
understand the relationship
between accepting Christ
as their Savior and being
forgiven for their sins. While
this session focuses on our
need for redemption, some
preteens may want to know
more about how to become
a Christian. Be sure to give
preteens the opportunity to
ask questions. Encourage
all preteens to be present
for the entire unit of study.

Session 2

He Died for Me?

FOCAL PASSAGES:
Romans 6:23; 5:8; Acts 3:19; Ephesians 2:8-9; Romans 10:9-10,13

MEMORY VERSE:
For the wages of sin is death, but the gift of God is eternal life in Christ Jesus our Lord. Romans 6:23

LIFE DESTINATION:
Preteens will understand that salvation is available to them only through personal faith in Christ as they repent of their sin, seek His forgiveness, and make Him the Lord of their lives.

How This Session Relates to Salvation

In this session, preteens will study Scripture passages that will lead them through the plan of salvation. Preteens will be given the opportunity to accept Christ as their personal Savior at the close of this session.

Bible Study for Leaders

Life is filled with decisions. Many of these decisions have significant consequences, even for preteens. Of all the decisions facing preteens, none is more significant than their choice to accept or reject God's gift of salvation through Jesus Christ.

God's Free Gift

From last week's session we know that "all have sinned" (Rom. 3:23). In Romans 6:23 Paul declared that the consequence of our sin is death. Paul explained more fully in Romans 5:12-14 how the problem of sin began with Adam and continues "because all sinned" (Rom 5:12). Though God is love (1 John 4:8), He is also just. He has declared that the punishment, the wage sin earns, is death (Rom. 1:32a). Therefore all people must die because all have sinned. The good news is that God in His mercy has provided a way for us to overcome death through the gift of His Son. Though we were sinners and undeserving of His mercy, God demonstrated His love for us by sending His Son to die for us as the sacrificial payment for our guilt as sinners (Rom. 5:8).

Saved by Grace Alone

Many people believe that hard work brings a reward in almost any endeavor. Unfortunately, some have tried to transfer this concept to the spiritual realm. They think that God will let them into heaven because they worked hard to do right. Paul made it clear in Ephesians 2:8-9 that we can never do enough good to earn God's salvation. God's redemption is a gift that He offers by His grace. Because redemption is a gift, no one can ever boast about working hard enough to achieve it.

What We Must Do

First, we must admit our sin problem and ask God to help us change direction, to repent (Acts 3:19). God's promise is that He will hear us, whoever we are, regardless of our sins. If we are serious and are ready to commit our lives to Him, God guarantees our salvation (Rom. 10:13). He forgives and cleanses us from our guilt (1 John 1:8-10) and enables us to start over.

The next step is to acknowledge publicly what we have done (Rom. 10:9-10). Because we make that commitment in our hearts, we are willing to confess Him openly. Then we are saved from our sin and receive from God the label "justified." This is the quality God requires of us before we can receive His gift of eternal life.

DISCUSS AND DO

GET READY

• Gather: pencils, wrapping paper, felt-tip marker, large sheet of paper, scissors, masking tape.
• Cut wrapping paper into four-inch squares. You will need one square for each student.

GET SET

• Attach the large sheet of paper to a focal wall.
• Arrange chairs in a circle.

GET STARTED

1. Identify characteristics of good gifts. As preteens arrive, give each one a pencil and a small square of wrapping paper. Instruct students to write on the plain side of the wrapping paper their favorite gift from last Christmas and three characteristics of a good gift.

When preteens have completed their assignment, invite volunteers to name their favorite gifts. Discuss the characteristics of a good gift. List the characteristics on the large sheet of paper. Circle the characteristics that are mentioned more than once. Stress that while we always enjoy receiving gifts, we appreciate some gifts more than others because of these characteristics. Tell preteens that in today's Bible study, they will discover some characteristics of the very best gift of all—eternal life.

DIG

GET READY

• Get these items from the resource box: foam hand, checkered flag, video.
• Gather: Bibles, *Preteen Handbooks*, wrapping paper, transparent tape, scissors, three large sheets of paper, marker.
• Secure: enough individually wrapped pieces of candy for each preteen present to have one, VCR and monitor.
• Cut out several copies of today's memory verse (Romans 6:23) from page 33 of the *Preteen Handbooks*. Cut each verse into several pieces. (You will need one piece for each preteen.)
• Tape each portion of the memory verse to a piece of candy. Create "gifts" by using additional wrapping paper to wrap each piece of candy.

GET SET

• Set up the VCR and monitor. Cue the video to the first segment, "What Is Grace, Anyway?"

GET STARTED

2. Learn a memory verse. Distribute candy "gifts." As preteens open their gifts, challenge them to complete the verse attached to their gift by connecting their portion of the verse with the portions distributed to other preteens. The first group to tape their pieces together wins. Wave the checkered flag and say, "Go."

Continue the game until everyone has completed the verse. Use the foam hand to point to the winners. Invite a

STEP 1

HINT

In order to keep the discussion of Christmas gifts from becoming a contest, focus on the gifts that have special meaning to the preteens. Remind preteens that good gifts are those that meet a need, are long-lasting, and are given out of love.

volunteer from that group to read aloud the memory verse (Romans 6:23). Point to students in other groups. Allow each of them to read aloud the memory verse.

Challenge preteens to repeat the first half of the verse from memory. *(For the wages of sin is death.)* Review the truths from last week's Bible study: (1) all have sinned; (2) because He is just, God must punish those who have sinned.

Challenge preteens to repeat the last half of the memory verse. *(But the gift of God is eternal life in Christ Jesus our Lord.)* Say: "God wants to give each of us a special gift, a gift to meet our deepest need."

Distribute *Preteen Handbooks.* Continue the examination of Romans 6:23 by asking preteens to help you compare the "wages of sin" with the "gift of God." Write "wages of sin =" and "gift of God =" on a large sheet of paper. Direct preteens to turn to page 9 in their *Preteen Handbooks* to review the first four entries in "Factionary." Ask: "What does Romans 6:23 say the wages of sin equal?" *(Death.)* "What does the gift of God equal?" *(Eternal life.)* Write the responses on the paper.

3. Define grace. Ask: "What does it take for a person to get to heaven?" Remind students that some people think good works can get them to heaven. Call for a volunteer to read aloud Ephesians 2:8-9. Call for another volunteer to read the definition of "saved" from "Factionary" on page 9 of the *Preteen Handbook.* Ask: "What

did Paul say is the relationship between good works and salvation?" *(We are saved through faith, not works.)*

Call for a volunteer to read the definition of "grace." Invite preteens to watch a video to determine what grace is and what grace is not.

Play each of the four segments of "What Is Grace, Anyway?" After each segment ask: "Was that an example of grace? Why or why not? How was this situation like—or unlike—God's grace?"

4. Determine the role of faith in salvation. Write on a second large sheet of paper the words "Me" and "God." Leave a space between the words. Write the word "Death" in the center beneath the phrases. Read aloud Ephesians 2:8. Call for a volunteer to complete this sentence: "We are saved through _____." *(Faith.)* Refer preteens to the definition of faith in "Factionary" on page 9 of the *Preteen Handbook.* Encourage preteens to give some examples of faith in everyday life. On the paper, draw an arching line from "Me" to "God." Write "Faith in Jesus Christ" above the line. Explain that God has offered the free gift of salvation through His Son Jesus. Our part in the process is to exercise faith. We must believe what God says and commit our lives to Him.

5. Determine characteristics of genuine love. Ask: "How do you know when someone genuinely loves you?" Write responses on a third large sheet of paper.

STEP
4

HINT

If preteens have trouble thinking of examples of faith from everyday life, mention one or more of these ideas: faith that a bridge will support my car; faith that a friend will keep my secret; faith that my family will supply my needs.

Read aloud Romans 5:8. Call for a volunteer to identify the evidence of God's love found in the passage. *(God sent His Son to die for us even though we are sinners.)*

6. Identify steps to salvation. Direct preteens' attention to the diagram with faith linking people to God. Explain that the Bible identifies several specific steps a person must take to cross that bridge of faith. Direct preteens to complete "Steps of Faith" on page 9 in the *Preteen Handbook.* After a few minutes, invite volunteers to share the steps. *(Answers: Acts 3:19–repent, turn to God; Romans 10:9-10–confess, believe; Romans 10:13–when we call on the name of the Lord, we will be saved.)*

DECIDE
GET READY
• Make enough copies of the bookmark on page 24 ("Stuff to Copy") so that each preteen present can have one.

GET STARTED
7. Examine "God's ABC's." Instruct preteens to find "God's ABC's" on page 10 of the *Preteen Handbook.* Explain that this page provides a simple outline of what a person needs to know and do to be saved. Review each step. Read aloud the definition of "repent" on page 9 of the *Preteen Handbook.* Encourage preteens to look up and mark in their Bibles each verse listed in the ABC's. Suggest that preteens write the ABC's along with the Scripture references and page numbers in the front of their Bibles. Remind preteens that they can use the ABC's and the Scriptures they have marked in their Bibles to tell someone how to become a Christian.

8. Respond to an opportunity to receive God's gift of salvation. Read aloud Romans 10:13. Tell preteens that they can respond to God's offer of salvation right now. Direct preteens attention to the prayer at the end of "God's ABC's." Encourage those who want to accept Jesus as Lord of their lives to read the prayer silently to God. Suggest that those who are already Christians review the plan of salvation so they can share it from memory.

Give each student a bookmark. Explain that Satan can limit our power as Christians if he can get us to doubt that we have been saved. Invite preteens to write on the bookmark their names and the date they accepted Christ as their Savior. Suggest that those who are not ready to make this decision write their names and birthdates on the bookmark to remind them that they are God's creation. Encourage preteens to keep the bookmark in their Bibles to remind them of their status as God's children.

Urge those who prayed today to receive God's gift to tell you, their parents, or another adult as soon as possible so they can receive counsel and encouragement. Close the session by thanking God for the gift of His Son.

STEP 7

HINT
Before the session, check your church records to see which preteens have not made public decisions to accept Christ. Pray especially for each of those preteens before the session. During the session, be particularly sensitive to any questions they might have.

After the session, schedule a time to talk further with any preteen who indicates she has prayed to receive Christ.

Session 3

I Can Be Victorious!

FOCAL PASSAGES:
Romans 7:18–8:2;
1 Corinthians 15:57-58

MEMORY VERSE:
Therefore, there is now no condemnation for those who are in Christ Jesus.
Romans 8:1

LIFE DESTINATION:
Preteens will understand the reality of the Christian's continuing struggle with sin and recognize that Jesus is their ally in this struggle.

How This Session Relates to Salvation

Some preteens may have misconceptions about becoming a Christian and living the Christian life. Examining Paul's testimony of his struggle to live out his faith in a consistent way can help preteens understand that becoming a Christian is only the beginning. Christian preteens will be challenged to a new way of living. Non-Christians will be encouraged to take that first step and accept Christ as their Savior.

Bible Study for Leaders

As preteens focus on the major truths surrounding God's salvation, they may assume that becoming a new person in Christ means not only the removal of the guilt of sin but also the loss of the desire to sin. Examining Paul's testimony in Romans 7 can help students see more clearly the true condition of believers.

The Battle Within

In Romans 7:18-20 Paul shared his struggle to live the way God wanted him to live. Even though Paul wanted to live in a way that was pleasing to God, he often found that he was unable to carry out his desire to please God. Paul realized that the problem was his human, sinful nature. While God had redeemed his soul, Paul still lived in a body of flesh, a body with desires and appetites that tried to ignore God's standards.

Paul came to understand that a war raged within his soul. The habit of sin in his life was so strong that he could not will himself to do the right thing. This inability to do what he knew he should do caused Paul to feel like a prisoner of war. He longed for someone to rescue him from his "wretched" condition and set him free.

Freedom through the Spirit

God enabled Paul to understand that through Jesus, he could be free from his guilt and the fear of death. Paul responded by accepting God's forgiveness and guarantee of eternal life. As Paul struggled with the influence of sin in his life after he became a Christian, he looked for a way to escape not only the guilt of sin but also its continuing power. Paul came to realize that when God saved him, He also freed him from sin's influence (Rom. 8:1-2). God did this by placing in Paul at the moment of his conversion the gift of His Spirit. In his own strength, Paul was still a prisoner of sin's influence. But, through the supernatural strength of God's Spirit, Paul had the ability to do what God wanted him to do.

Victory!

Paul stressed that Jesus' resurrection is the basis for our hope. Since we believe that God raised Jesus from the dead, we also believe that God will enable us to live beyond the death of our physical bodies. Through God's power in our lives we can have victory over the power of sin each day and even at the moment we face physical death.

DISCUSS AND DO

GET READY

• Get this item from the resource box: checkered flag.
• Gather: scissors, four or five large envelopes, *Preteen Handbooks*.
• Secure: three or four large squares of craft foam of various colors.
• Create puzzles by cutting large squares of craft foam into irregular shapes. You will need one puzzle for every four to five preteens expected. Place all but one of the puzzle pieces for each set in a large envelope. Keep the other pieces in a separate envelope.

GET SET

• Arrange chairs in circles of four to five chairs each. Place a puzzle envelope in the center of each circle.

GET STARTED

1. Experience frustration. As preteens arrive, invite them to be seated in one of the circles of chairs and to begin work on assembling the puzzle in the envelope. Allow each group to work long enough to realize that they cannot complete their puzzle with the pieces they have been given. Express your surprise and offer to help. Give each group their missing puzzle piece.

After the groups have completed their puzzles, encourage them to describe their frustration as they tried to put together the puzzle with a piece missing. Remind pre-

teens that sometimes we encounter problems in life that frustrate us as well.

2. Identify examples of frustration. Direct preteens to remain in their small groups. Assign each group one of the case studies on page 12 of the *Preteen Handbook*. Instruct the groups to discuss the struggle depicted in the case study. Encourage each group to think of some additional examples of struggles preteens face.

After about five minutes, use the checkered flag to call time. Call on a volunteer from each group to report on their assigned case study. After all groups have reported, ask: "What are some other struggles preteens face?"

Tell preteens that in today's Bible study they will discover what Paul said about his own struggle with sin and they will learn how they can have both the desire and the ability to honor Christ everyday.

DIG

GET READY

• Get this item from the resource box: key.
• Gather: Bibles, Preteen Handbooks, two or three rolls of black crepe paper streamers, scissors, masking tape.
• Cut a copy of today's memory verse (Romans 8:1) from page 33 of the *Preteen Handbook* for each preteen present. Tape one copy of the verse to the key.

STEP 2

HINT

Assign an adult leader to each group to guide the reading and discussion of the case studies.

A group may be assigned more than one case study if you have less than three groups. Two different groups can discuss the same case study if you have more than three groups.

GET SET

• Cut the black crepe paper into strips long enough to reach from ceiling to floor. Use masking tape to attach the strips to the ceiling. Strips should be about six inches apart and approximately two feet out from a wall. Hang enough strips so that three or four preteens can stand behind them.

GET STARTED

3. Identify Paul's problem.

Invite preteens to join you in forming a large circle. Remind preteens that Paul was one of the greatest Christians that ever lived, but he had a problem. Instruct preteens to read Romans 7:18 in their Bibles and the first entry in "Factionary" on page 11 of the *Preteen Handbook* to identify Paul's problem. *(Paul had the desire, but not the ability to do what is right.)* Encourage preteens to suggest some times when preteens might have the desire to do something, but not the ability. *(Possible responses: to make straight A's, to be a starter on the basketball team, to excel in playing a musical instrument.)* Ask: "How would someone feel who has a great desire to excel in a certain area but not the ability?" *(Possible responses: frustrated, angry, sad, depressed.)*

4. Visualize how Paul felt.

Call for three or four volunteers to stand behind the strips of black crepe paper that you have hung from the ceiling. Read aloud Romans 7:19-24. Ask: "How did Paul feel because of his inability to do what he knew was right?" *(He felt like a prisoner.)*

Direct preteens' attention to the second and third entries in the "Factionary" on page 11 of the *Preteen Handbook*. Briefly summarize Paul's condition: (1) he had a strong desire to honor God and do what he knew was right; (2) when he tried to do what was right, he found that he did not have the ability; (3) as a result of his inability to live consistently for God, he felt like sin's prisoner. Say: "Paul could have given up and just assumed that living a consistent Christian life was impossible."

Call for a volunteer to read aloud Romans 7:25–8:2. Pass the key through the crepe paper "bars." Instruct each preteen standing behind the bars to take the key, read aloud the memory verse, then walk through the bars. Give each preteen a memory verse card as she walks through the bars. Invite another group of preteens to stand behind the bars and do the same.

Invite preteens to be seated in the circle. Call for a volunteer to read aloud 1 Corinthians 15:57 and the last two entries in "Factionary" on page 11 of the *Preteen Handbook*. Ask: "How does knowing that you have this special freedom through Christ make you feel?" *(Possible responses: relieved, happy, grateful.)* Invite volunteers to offer aloud brief sentence prayers, thanking God for what He has done for us.

5. Determine what Christians should do with their freedom in Christ.

Call for a volunteer to help

STEP 4

HINT

Cut the shape of a lock from a large sheet of poster board. Draw a keyhole in the center of the lock and write the word "sin" above the keyhole. Choose a volunteer to serve as jailkeeper. Direct the jailkeeper to stand by the jail and hold the lock. As preteens read the memory verse aloud, instruct them to touch the key to the lock before exiting. When all preteens have been freed, tear the poster in half to symbolize their victory over sin.

you with an experiment. Instruct the student to stand on one foot with his arms stretched out. Tell the student to try to maintain his balance as two leaders pull his arms in opposite directions. After the leaders pull the student off balance, instruct the student to stand with both feet on the floor and slightly apart. Direct the leaders to try again to pull him off balance. After a few moments of pulling, ask preteens which position better enabled the student to maintain his balance.

Direct preteens to read 1 Corinthians 15:58 to discover what Paul said we should do in order to maintain our spiritual balance. Ask: "What did Paul say we should do?" *(Stand firm and let nothing move us.)* Invite preteens to suggest ways they can follow Paul's advice to "give yourselves fully to the work of the Lord." *(Possible responses: pray, read His Word, obey His commands.)*

DECIDE

GET READY

• Gather: Bibles, pencils, *Preteen Handbooks*, one sheet of notebook paper for each preteen present.

GET STARTED

6. Identify steps people can take to maintain freedom in Christ. Tell preteens that the Bible provides several steps we can take to maintain our freedom once we have accepted God's gift of salvation. Instruct the students to complete "Steps to Freedom" on page 11 of the

Preteen Handbook. (Answers: 1. struggle; 2. Thank; 3. stand firm; 4. Give yourselves fully; 5. Test, good; 6. prayer, petition, thanksgiving.) After two or three minutes, call for volunteers to share their findings.

Remind the preteens of Paul's struggle to live as a Christian and the victory he found through Christ.

Give each preteen a piece of notebook paper. Encourage students to write a brief prayer, asking God to help them in some specific ways to live lives that are free from the power of sin. As preteens finish writing, suggest that they read their prayers silently to God.

Dismiss.

STEP 5

HINT

If preteens have difficulty thinking of ways to give themselves fully to the Lord, suggest appropriate ways preteens can be involved in Christian service, such as participating in church music activities for their age group, being involved in mission activities offered by your church, or giving to the church a tithe of the money they receive as allowances or earnings.

Session 4

A Brand New Me

FOCAL PASSAGE:
Romans 12:1-21

MEMORY VERSE:
Therefore, I urge you, brothers, in view of God's mercy, to offer your bodies as living sacrifices, holy and pleasing to God—this is your spiritual act of worship. Romans 12:1

LIFE DESTINATION:
Preteens will understand the difference that Christ's transforming power can make in a Christian's life and will discover how they can experience that power in their own lives.

How This Session Relates to Salvation

When we talk about evangelism and conversion, we often emphasize the elements closely connected with the decision to accept Christ. But, in fact, a decision to accept Christ as Savior and Lord is only the beginning point of Christian conversion. We can help preteens better understand salvation as we describe the life-long process of being transformed into the likeness of Christ.

Bible Study for Leaders

If a person travels a hundred miles before he discovers that he is going in the wrong direction, he must make a major adjustment to recover from the error. The time and effort required to correct the mistake is much less for someone who realizes his error after traveling only five miles. Preteens do not have a long way to go in adjusting to following Christ—they have not been on the journey very long. For Christian preteens the transformation is a change in focus, a learning of new guideposts that provide direction for the journey. In Romans 12 the apostle Paul outlines the goal of the Christian's journey. He provides specific guideposts to help believers stay on the right road.

New Life in Christ

In his struggle to obey God's will, Paul came to view himself as someone who had died. Dead men have no desires or rights. Paul described himself as one who was "always being given over to death" (2 Cor. 4:11). He used this same image in Romans 12:1 when he urged his readers to offer themselves to God as "living sacrifices." This act of worship meant that they were to give up all their rights in order to serve God. In the process they would be "transformed."

In this process of transformation, some of us may progress faster than others. We may be tempted to think we are superior to other believers. Paul recognized this danger and warned the Christians in Rome not to "think of yourself more highly than you ought" (12:3). God has given each of us different gifts and abilities. He has placed us in the body of Christ to serve one another.

New Rules for Life

The key question for the game of life is not, "Are there any rules?" but "Which set of rules do we follow?" Everyone plays by some set of rules. For the Christian all the rules revolve around one theme: love. In Romans 12:9-21, Paul emphasized that life is to be lived under the banner of love. Genuine love puts others first, shares with those in need, blesses instead of curses, tries to live in harmony and peace, and leaves vengeance to God. God's people are to be humble and hospitable and involved with others in both their joys and their sorrows. Love is active both in doing good and in resisting evil. Those who focus on serving the Lord in a spirit of love will be joyful as they anticipate the future.

DISCUSS AND DO

GET READY
• Get these items from the resource box: foam hand, checkered flag.
• Gather: a large sheet of paper, marker, tape.

GET SET
• Move all chairs against the wall to leave the center of the room unobstructed.
• Write this command on the large sheet of paper: "Walk around the room." Post the command on a focal wall.

GET STARTED
1. Participate in an experiment. Greet preteens as they arrive by using the foam hand to point to the command written on the large sheet of paper. (Adult leaders should avoid answering questions or providing any further explanation. They should stand near the door or against a wall.) Encourage arriving students to join the others in following the command.

After a few minutes, quietly enlist two preteens to walk together in any pattern they choose as long as they do it together.

After two or three more minutes, wave the checkered flag and direct students to form groups of three or four. Instruct preteens to tell one another how they felt about the activity and what, if any, pressure they felt to conform in the way they walked or acted. Invite volunteers from each group to report their feelings about the need to

conform. Remind preteens that there are more ways to conform than by just copying what someone else does. They may have conformed in their attitudes. (If some thought the activity was fun, others probably agreed. If some thought the activity was silly, others probably agreed.) Highlight any instances you observed where preteens conformed in the way they interacted with each other.

Ask: "What are some examples from daily life when you feel pressure to conform? How are you affected when you conform to the influence of others?"

DIG

GET READY
• Enlist a preteen to portray a dead person lying on a table.
• Get these items from the resource box: checkered flag, Poster 1.
• Copy and cut apart "Qualities of a Transformed Life" on page 24 ("Stuff to Copy").
• Gather: Bibles, *Preteen Handbooks*, pencils, some small artificial flowers, a bedsheet, a large sheet of paper, bright-colored wrapping paper and a bow, small box, two to three sheets of notebook paper for each preteen, paper sack, enough folders so that each preteen present can have one, an assortment of household items. (See HINT Step 4, page 23.)
• Secure: a highlighter for each preteen present, a large table sturdy enough for a preteen to lie on.

STEP 1

HINT

For examples of ways we encounter pressure to conform, suggest these ideas: when someone starts "the wave" at a sporting event; when someone starts to applaud or stand; when someone starts to yawn or cough; when your friends want to go somewhere you don't feel comfortable going.

• Place household items in the paper sack.

• Wrap the small box with bright-colored wrapping paper and tie with a bow.

• Prepare a folder for each student by placing two or three sheets of notebook paper behind a letter addressed specifically to each student in which you suggest possible spiritual gifts you see in the student.

GET SET

• Set the large table in the front of the room. Cover the table with the bedsheet.

• Attach Poster 1 to the focal wall.

GET STARTED

2. Determine the qualities of a dead person. Instruct the previously enlisted preteen to lie on the table and pretend to be dead. Provide artificial flowers for the student to hold. Encourage the other students to form a circle around the "dead" body. Challenge preteens name aloud the qualities of a dead person. Enlist a volunteer to write responses on the large sheet of paper. *(Possible responses: They don't move, they don't breath, they don't feel anything.)* After several qualities have been mentioned, elaborate on the qualities that suggest that the dead person has no rights or feelings. Invite preteens to be seated.

Instruct the preteen lying on the table to sit up. Give him a Bible and ask him to read aloud Romans 12:1-2. Discuss the irony of "living sacrifices." Instruct preteens to read the first three entries in "Factionary" on page 13 of

the *Preteen Handbook.* Ask: "What was Paul urging the Christians to do?" *(Put God first, choose to act the way God would act.)*

Remind preteens of the discussion on conformity they had earlier. Ask: "What kind of conformity did Paul urge the believers to avoid?" *(Conformity to this world.)* "What alternative did he propose?" *(Be transformed, do God's will.)* Conclude the discussion of this passage by clarifying that those who offer themselves to God as sacrifices are giving God the offering He most desires.

3. Identify spiritual gifts. Display the small wrapped package. Enlist an adult leader to read aloud Romans 12:3-8. Call for a volunteer to read the fourth and fifth entries in "Factionary" on page 13 of the *Preteen Handbook.* Read the first sentence from verse 6 again. Tell preteens that every believer has a spiritual gift from God.

Instruct preteens to complete "Clues about Gifts" on page 14 of the *Preteen Handbook.* As the students work on the assignment, give each student his or her personalized spiritual gifts notebook. (Remember to give visitors a notebook with a letter of welcome included.)

When preteens have finished marking their responses, instruct them to determine their scores according to the directions in the *Preteen Handbook.* Tell preteens to write the area of interest that has the highest score in the space provided. Suggest that they consider

STEP 3

HINT

Before the session, prepare several extra notebooks for visitors by writing letters of welcome to those students. As visitors arrive, assign an adult leader to write each visitor's name on an extra notebook.

the possibility that the item with the highest score may be their spiritual gift.

Allow preteens a moment to read the letter in the notebooks you have distributed. Encourage preteens to exchange notebooks and write on the blank paper the gifts they see in each other. Remind them that they can look at the list of gifts in the *Preteen Handbook* for ideas.

Invite preteens to pause for a minute to thank God for the gifts He has given them. Conclude the prayer time by thanking God aloud for the gifts He has given each of the students.

4. Create a symbol. Call attention to the butterfly on Poster 1. Discuss how a caterpillar is transformed into a beautiful butterfly. Remind preteens that we, too, can be transformed when we do what God wants us to do.

Read aloud Romans 12:11 and the last entry in "Factionary" on page 13 of the *Preteen Handbook.* Give each student one of the qualities copied from "Qualities of a Transformed Life." Spread on the floor the contents of the paper sack. Instruct preteens to use the materials provided to create a symbol for their assigned quality. Wave the checkered flag to begin the activity. (Adult leaders should be available to interpret and define the qualities as needed.)

As the students finish their creations, instruct them to complete "Do's and Don't's" on page 13 of the *Preteen Handbook* by highlighting the actions Paul encouraged the believers to do and drawing a line through the actions Paul urged the believers to avoid.

When preteens have completed the assignment, call for volunteers to name some of the things Paul said we should avoid. Say: "Let's look at the symbols you have created to remind us of some things Paul said we should do." Call for volunteers to interpret their creations.

DECIDE
GET READY

• Gather: shoe box, pencils, enough half sheets of paper so that each student present can have one.
• Write on the inside of the lid of the shoe box: "Rest in Peace."

GET SET
• Place the shoe box on a table with the lid standing upright so that the words "Rest in Peace" are visible.

GET STARTED
5. Demonstrate the memory verse. Give each student a sheet of paper. Read aloud the memory verse (Romans 12:1). Challenge students to write one thing he or she will do this week to live a transformed life. Remind preteens that in order to live transformed lives, they have to "die" to their own selfish desires. Instruct preteens to fold their paper in half and drop it into the shoebox "grave." Form a large circle around the "grave." Close in prayer asking God to help preteens live transformed lives.

Stuff to Copy

Session 1, Step 6

Get into Heaven Ticket

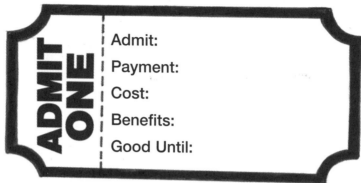

ADMIT ONE

Admit:

Payment:

Cost:

Benefits:

Good Until:

Session 2, Step 7

NAME:

DATE:

Session 4, Step 4
Qualities of a Transformed Life

Copy and cut apart the following qualities. Give one or more slips to each preteen.

expresses genuine love	blesses those who persecute you
attracted to good	rejoices with those who rejoice
hate what is evil	mourns with those who mourn
devoted to one another in brotherly love	lives in harmony with others
honors others above self	not proud or conceited
full of zeal and spiritual fervor	doesn't repay evil for evil
serving the Lord	careful to do what is right
joyful in hope	tries to live at peace with everyone
patient in affliction	does not try to get revenge
faithful in prayer	is kind his/her enemies
shares with those in need	tries to avoid being overcome by evil
hospitable	tries to overcome evil with good

UNIT 2

Pass It On!

Session 1: Listen Up!

Focal Passages: Acts 1:8; 8:26-38; 1 Corinthians 15:3-4
Life Destination: Preteens will become aware of opportunities to share Christ as they realize their responsibility to share the good news of salvation.
Memory Verse: You will be his witness to all men of what you have seen and heard. *Acts 22:15*

Session 2: Watch Me!

Focal Passages: Matthew 5:13-16; 25:31-46
Life Destination: Preteens will share Christ's love by ministering to others.
Memory Verse: Let your light shine before men, that they may see your good deeds and praise your Father in heaven. *Matthew 5:16*

Unit Direction

Preteens will learn the importance of sharing Christ through their words and their deeds.

Session 1
Listen Up!

How This Session Relates to Salvation

The Bible often refers to believers as stewards. Besides being accountable for the stewardship of material things, believers are also accountable for what they do with the good news of salvation. To be good stewards, Christian preteens must always be sharing the gospel with those who have not yet heard.

Bible Study for Leaders

Throughout humanity's existence God has tried to communicate His message of love to us. God delivered His boldest message through His Son, Jesus. God could have used complex schemes to report the story of Jesus' ministry. Instead, He chose to limit His message to the witness of those who have experienced His gift of salvation. After Jesus came out of the tomb, and before He returned to heaven, He announced His Father's plan (Acts 1:8). First, God would give each believer the gift of His Holy Spirit. The Spirit would then enable the Christian to communicate in a powerful way to those who had not yet heard God's good news.

Look for Opportunities

The account in Acts 8:26-38 of Philip's witness to an Ethiopian official is a perfect example of how God intended His communication plan to work. God sent a special messenger, an angel, to convince Philip to leave a spiritual harvest time in Samaria. Philip obeyed the angel's message and went to the desert road that led from Jerusalem to Gaza. As he walked along the road, Philip realized that God wanted him to walk near a particu-lar chariot. The chariot belonged to a government official from Ethiopia who was on his way home after worshipping God in Jerusalem.

As Philip walked beside the chariot, he heard the official reading aloud. Philip perceived that the man was reading from a scroll of the Book of Isaiah. The passage he was reading was Isaiah 53:7-8. Philip boldly, but politely, asked the man if he understood what he was reading. The man indicated his need for someone to interpret and invited Philip to join him in the chariot. Philip used the man's questions to share with him the good news about Jesus. The man believed and asked to be baptized.

Share the Good News

Just as Philip carried out Jesus' commission to witness, so did many other early Christians. Among the most dedicated and effective witnesses was the apostle Paul. After a life-changing encounter with Jesus, Paul's focus was to share the good news of salvation. Paul always kept the message simple: Jesus proved He was God's Son and fulfilled Old Testament prophecies by dying on the cross and rising from the dead three days later. (See 1 Corinthians 15:3-4.) This was the message Paul shared in Corinth that resulted in many coming to a faith relationship with Christ.

DISCUSS AND DO
GET READY

• Gather: pencils, several sheets of paper for each team of four to six preteens.

• Provide enough donuts so that each preteen present can have one.

• Make one copy of the "Group Assignment" on page 34 ("Stuff to Copy") for every four to six preteens present.

GET SET

• Arrange chairs in groups of four to six. Place these items in the center of each circle of chairs: a pencil, several sheets of paper, a copy of the group instructions.

• Set the donuts out of sight.

GET STARTED

1. Develop an escape plan. As students arrive, invite them to join a group and begin working on the assignment you have placed in the center of the circle of chairs. Quietly show one of the arriving students the location of the donuts and explain that he or she may have one. Do not say anything else about the donuts. Simply allow preteens to "spread the word" about the donuts themselves.

When preteens have completed their assignment, call for a volunteer from each group to share their escape plan. Say: "It is important to know how to escape a burning building. It is even more important to know how to escape the consequence of sin."

Call attention to the donuts. Determine how many preteens got one and how they found out where they were. *(They told each other.)* Emphasize that only one student knew about the donuts at the beginning of the session. Tell preteens that that God has a similar communication plan for letting the whole world know about His offer of forgiveness and salvation.

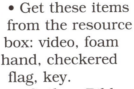

DIG
GET READY

• Get these items from the resource box: video, foam hand, checkered flag, key.

• Gather: Bibles, pencils, *Preteen Handbooks*, three large paper sacks, an assortment of common household items such as a remote control, magazines, paper plates, pens, pencils, blankets or pillows, packages of tissue, computer disks, books, and so on.

• Place an assortment of household items in each of the three paper sacks.

• Collect several items that represent a plan or a sequence. (See HINT, Step 6, page 29, for suggestions.)

• Secure a VCR and monitor.

• Make a copy of the "Opportunity Guide" from "Stuff to Copy" on page 34 for each student present.

GET SET

• Set up the VCR and monitor. Cue the video to the beginning of the second segment, "The Play-by-Play."

STEP 1

HINT

If after a couple of minutes, no one has asked the student with the donut the location of the refreshments, quietly whisper to the student that he or she may let others know about the donuts.

STEP

3

HINT

Elements of Philip's effectiveness as a witness might include: his willingness to be guided by God's Spirit, his concern for people who were different from himself, his willingness to listen, his boldness, his confidence in his message, his knowledge of the Bible, his understanding of what a person must do in order to be saved.

2. Personalize Acts 1:8. Direct preteens to move their chairs to form one large circle. Call for a volunteer to explain briefly the reason Christians celebrate Easter Sunday. *(Because Jesus rose from the dead.)* Call for volunteers to share how they found out about Easter. *(Someone told them. They read about it.)* Say: "Everything we know about Jesus—His birth, His life, His death, His resurrection, His promise to return—we know because someone told someone else, either in person or through the written word. Since Jesus wanted everyone to know what He had done for them, He commissioned His followers to be His witnesses. He wanted them to tell others what they knew from their own experiences."

Guide preteens to personalize Jesus' commission by referring them to "My Personal Assignment" on page 15 of the *Preteen Handbook*.

As students finish writing, call for several volunteers to read aloud their personalized versions of Acts 1:8. Explain that as we receive God's gift of salvation through Jesus and experience the benefits of a personal relationship with God, then we can tell others how to become a Christian.

GET STARTED
3. Develop mini-dramas. Refer the students to "Acts 8 x Today" on page 16 of the *Preteen Handbook*. Form three groups with an adult leader in each group. Assign one section of the activity to each group. Give each group one of the bags of assorted

household objects and one of the gadgets from the resource box. Direct preteens to use the materials provided to prepare a contemporary drama of the section assigned to them. Tell preteens that they will have ten minutes to prepare their presentations. Their presentations should be no longer than three minutes each.

Encourage the students to refer to "Factionary" on page 15 of the *Preteen Handbook* for a better understanding of some of the key terms and ideas in Acts 8:26-38.

When the students have completed their assignment, call on each group, in the appropriate sequence, to present its mini-drama. After all have shared, invite volunteers to describe the specific elements of Philip's witness.

4. Identify witnessing opportunities. Give each student a copy of the "Opportunity Guide." Instruct preteens to respond to the first two questions. Encourage preteens to keep in mind the witness of Philip as they work.

After about three minutes, call for volunteers to share their responses to questions 1 and 2. Affirm and clarify responses as needed. Direct preteens to set their "Opportunity Guides" aside for now.

5. Watch a video. Explain that the following video segment uses instant replay to help us better understand how to see and respond to opportunities to be witnesses. Show the video segment, "The Play-by-Play." Call for volunteers to identify from the video specific examples of seeing an opportunity and ways of responding.

Stress that our witness begins with the way we show others the reality and power of God's love through our daily activities. Continue by emphasizing that while living a good life is crucial to being an effective witness, simply *being* good is not enough. Remind preteens that in order for persons to know about Jesus and the salvation He offers, they have to be told. Remind the preteens that God's plan for how people will be told is found in Acts 1:8.

6. Focus on God's plan.

Distribute among the students some or all of the items you have collected that in some way represents a plan or sequence.

After preteens have had an opportunity to examine several of the items, call for a volunteer to name some things that the items have in common. Affirm responses that relate to a plan or planning. Call for volunteers to suggest reasons for having a plan.

Say: "God saw that the people He had created had a problem called sin, so He developed a plan to provide a solution." Instruct preteens to complete "A Gospel Summary" on page 16 in the *Preteen Handbook* to discover some key elements of God's plan.

After five minutes or so, wave the checkered flag to call time. Call for volunteers to share their answers. (*Answers: 1. died, Scriptures; 2. buried; 3. raised,*

Scriptures.) Call for a volunteer to read aloud Isaiah 53:5-6. Call for another volunteer to read aloud Psalm 16:9-10. Ask: "How did Jesus fulfill these Old Testament Scriptures?" (*He died for our sins and was raised from the dead.*) Remind preteens that God sent Jesus to carry out His plan to provide a solution to our sin problem.

DECIDE
GET STARTED
7. Determine one person to whom they can be a witness. Call for several volunteers to read aloud Acts 22:15. Challenge preteens to repeat the verse from memory. Refer preteens to the "Opportunity Guide" they worked on earlier. Instruct preteens to complete questions 3 through 5.

When preteens have completed their assignment, encourage them to circle at least one name from those they listed that they will make an effort to witness to this week.

After a few minutes, lead in prayer, asking God to help preteens discover opportunities to witness to the person whose name they circled. Dismiss.

STEP 6

HINT
If preteens need help thinking of reasons for having a plan, mention these: makes for more efficient use of time, enables one to do a better job, can lessen frustration with a difficult task.

STEP 6

HINT
Items that represent a plan or sequence might include: blueprints or copies of house plans from magazines, a map with a route marked, a calendar with several entries, copies of actual students' school schedules, copies of your church's budget, or copies of your church's order of service.

STEP 7

HINT
Encourage preteens to use the "Opportunity Guide" and "A Gospel Summary" (page 16, *Preteen Handbook*) to develop a plan for sharing the gospel with their friends. Remind preteens that they might want to include Romans 10:9-10,13 in their presentations of the plan of salvation.

Session 2
Watch Me!

FOCAL PASSAGES:
Matthew 5:13-16;
25:31-46

MEMORY VERSE:
Let your light shine
before men, that they
may see your good
deeds and praise your
Father in heaven.
Matthew 5:16

LIFE DESTINATION:
Preteens will share
Christ's love by minister-
ing to others.

How This Session Relates to Salvation

Some people teach that evangelism can only be viewed as a direct verbal witness. Others say that social ministry is the only true way to reach a hurting world. The content of this study can help pre-teens see that Jesus' way is not either/or but both. Jesus' way is a demonstration of caring that points directly to the source of the love that motivates and empowers.

Bible Study for Leaders

As Christians, Jesus calls us to be different, but not merely for the sake of being different. Rather, His goal is for His followers to use their distinctiveness to influence others and point them to the unchanging truth that resides in God the Father. One of the fundamental distinctives of the Christian way is the sharing of Christ's love by ministering to others.

In His Sermon on the Mount (Matt. 5:13-16), Jesus compared the distinctive influence of the Christian to salt and light. In both comparisons, He stressed the waste and loss of value if either element failed to fulfill its intended purpose. Salt that has lost its ability to season is useless and thus worthless. People do not waste light by covering it, but rather place it where it can provide the most effective illumination.

Jesus urged His disciples to be living lights who, by their examples, provide guidance to those around them. Their light was to be not merely words, but actual deeds lived out in the real world, in the midst of real trials and tribulations. Lives that consistently reflect love and peace and power through the hard times get others' attention.

I Can Share by Serving

Perhaps the most distinctive feature of the Christian way is the goal of following the Master in servanthood. Jesus both taught and lived the standard of putting others' needs ahead of our own.

In one of His teachings (Matt. 25:31-46) Jesus portrayed a sharp contrast between the servant's way and the way of those who seek to be served. An amazing fact stands out in this picture of the final judgment. When the Son of Man looks at people to see who are His and who are not, the most defining characteristic He observes is the presence or absence of a servant spirit. Though Jesus could have highlighted many other qualities and achievements, He said He will recognize His true followers by their servant hearts. Jesus was not saying that good deeds determine one's eternal fate, but rather that good deeds indicate the condition of one's heart which does determine one's eternal fate.

As we live out the life Christ has put in those of us who have received Him, we will naturally share His love by serving others.

DISCUSS AND DO

GET READY

• Gather: pencils, *Preteen Handbooks*, marker, three sheets of blank paper.

• Write each of the following on a blank sheet of paper: Case Study 1, Case Study 2, Case Study 3.

• Prepare an unsalted snack—something that is usually eaten salted such as chips, peanuts, or popcorn. Provide small paper cups or napkins for serving the snacks.

GET SET

• Arrange chairs in three circles. Place a case study assignment on the floor in the center of each circle. Place pencils and *Preteen Handbooks* on chairs.

GET STARTED

1. Analyze case studies. Welcome preteens as they arrive, and direct them to one of the three circles of chairs. Invite preteens to find "Good Deeds" on page 18 of their *Preteen Handbooks*. Instruct preteens to work as a team to review their assigned case study. Circulate among the groups with unsalted snacks.

After a few minutes, invite volunteers from each group to describe the act of ministry, the attitude of the person performing the act, and the possible effects on the person receiving the ministry. Follow up by encouraging preteens to share some particular acts of kindness done to them. Invite those who respond to explain why they are able to recall these particular acts and how these acts affected them. Tell preteens that today's Bible study focuses on how we can extend Christ's love through acts of ministry.

DIG

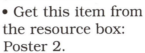

GET READY

• Get this item from the resource box: Poster 2.

• Gather: Bibles, pencils, *Preteen Handbooks*.

• Secure: a small houseplant or flower; a flashlight and a small bucket large enough to cover the flashlight, a large sheet of paper.

GET SET

• Arrange chairs in one large circle.

• Attach Poster 2 to the focal wall.

GET STARTED

2. Relate the effect of salt and light to the influence of Christians. Pass the unsalted snacks around the large circle again. Call for volunteers to suggest why these snacks taste a little different. *(They are unsalted.)* Continue by encouraging volunteers to discuss how salt affects the taste of foods.

Hold up the small plant. Ask: "What would happen if we put this plant in a dark room for several weeks?" *(It would die.)* "How much light would it take to keep this plant alive?" *(The light from a small bulb would be enough to keep the plant alive.)* Call for volunteers to discuss the importance of light.

STEP 1

HINT

Enlist an older teenager to share a time when someone was kind to him when he was a preteen. Encourage the teen to discuss how important that kindness was to him and how it made him feel. End the discussion time with a challenge to preteens to think about how their actions affect others.

STEP 3

HINT

In dealing with the rewards section of the chart, be sensitive to possible negative reactions to the fate of the unrighteous. Be careful to affirm the reality pictured by Jesus while reminding preteens of God's love and His desire that all accept His offer of forgiveness and salvation. Offer to talk later with anyone who is interested in discussing these concepts further.

Direct preteens to find Matthew 5:13-16 in their Bibles. Instruct preteens to silently read the passage to discover what Jesus said about the effectiveness of salt and light.

Turn on the flashlight and stand where everyone can see. Place the bucket over the flashlight. Ask: "How does this action relate to what Jesus said about light? In the passage you read, how did Jesus compare Christians to light?"

Call attention to Poster 2. Lead preteens in saying the session's memory verse (Matt. 5:16) aloud together from the poster. Call for volunteers to identify what this verse says about the reason Jesus wanted His followers to be involved in doing good deeds. *(So they could point others to God.)* Remind preteens that when they live the way God wants them to live, they will have the opportunity to be salt and light for Him as they quietly influence others to see the difference God's presence can make in a person's life.

3. Identify the actions of and the rewards for Jesus' followers. Remind preteens that Jesus placed a great deal of emphasis on the ministry of His followers. Instruct preteens to complete the chart in "Sorting and Separating" on page 18 of the *Preteen Handbook* to analyze what Jesus said about ministry. Encourage students to refer to the entries in "Factionary" on page 17 of the *Preteen Handbook* for additional information about the Scripture.

As preteens complete their charts, call for volunteers to share their findings. Challenge preteens to decide if the following statement is *true* or *false*: "In Matthew 5:31-46 Jesus teaches that performing acts of ministry is the basis for receiving eternal life." *(False.)* Invite students to share their responses and explain their reasoning.

Use information found in the "Bible Study for Leaders," page 30, to remind preteens that good deeds are evidence of a personal relationship with Christ, but they are not the basis for God's deciding who enters heaven. The only way to get into heaven is through a faith response to the salvation available to us through Jesus. Good deeds merely reflect what is in our hearts.

DECIDE

GET READY

• Gather: *Preteen Handbooks*, pencils, three large sheets of paper, masking tape, three markers.

GET SET

• Move chairs into three large circles.

GET STARTED

4. Develop a ministry guide. Remind preteens that even though we want to be effective ministers for Jesus' sake, there will be times when we need some guidance. Invite preteens to form again the three teams in which they worked at the beginning of the session. Give each team a large sheet of paper and a felt-tip marker. Instruct each team to develop a list of ministry ideas in which preteens could be involved.

After about five minutes, invite each team to attach their response sheet to a focal wall. Call for a spokesperson from each group to read their list aloud. When all the lists have been shared, encourage preteens to point out similarities among the lists and to suggest additional ideas that are generated through the reports.

Say: "The kind of service that most pleases Jesus is ministry that comes simply from seeing a need and responding." Challenge the students to focus on their relationship with Jesus as they go through each day so that they will be ready to respond to the opportunities Jesus places along their routes.

5. Complete a letter from Jesus. Remind preteens of the three case studies examined at the beginning of the session. Refer to the lists of ideas attached to the focal wall. Direct preteens to "A Letter from Jesus" on page 17 of the *Preteen Handbook.* Encourage preteens to imagine that this is a real letter from Jesus. Instruct them to use the ideas that have been shared to list ways they have been involved in serving and or could be involved in serving others.

After a few minutes, remind preteens of the emphasis Jesus placed on His followers having servant hearts that result in unselfish service to others. Encourage preteens to consider anything that might tend to limit their effectiveness as ministers for Christ. Invite volunteers to name some of these potential barriers. *(Possible answers: concern over what others might think; not enough time; concern about how a person might respond; not sure I would do the right thing.)* Acknowledge the reality of these possible barriers, but remind students that God's help is available to us to overcome anything that might stand in the way of our following Jesus' example of servanthood.

Lead preteens to bow their heads. Encourage them to focus on the things they wrote in their "Letter from Jesus." Guide preteens to think of any barriers that might keep them from serving others. Suggest that preteens pray silently as they ask God's help to enable them to be effective ministers.

Close the session by thanking God for Jesus' example of ministry and asking that God enable us all to follow His example.

STEP 5

HINT

Suggest two or three possible ministry projects that preteens could be involved in as a group. Guide preteens to choose one project and make plans to be a part of that ministry.

Possible ministry projects might include: gathering food for the church's food pantry, visiting a nursing home, feeding the homeless, or doing yard work for someone who is homebound.

Stuff to Copy

For use in Session 1, Step 1.
Make one copy of these instructions for every four to six preteens present.

Group Assignment

Work as a group to develop a communication plan to tell anyone who might be in the building how to escape in the case of an emergency, such as a fire. The communication plan should provide instructions that can be understood by non-readers as well as by those who do not speak English. Your plan should include alternate routes.

Make a copy of this guide for each student to use in Session 1, Steps 4 and 7.

Opportunity Guide

Answer the following questions to help you recognize opportunities to witness.

1. What are some conversation topics that I could use to introduce the need or benefits of a personal relationship with God? (Ex. The death of a loved one.)

2. What are some questions I could use to help determine if someone is a Christian? (Example: What do you think it takes for a person to go to heaven?)

3. Whom do I see regularly who, as far as I know, is not a Christian?

4. Whom do I know well enough to discuss serious issues with, such as personal spiritual beliefs?

5. Whom do I know who appears to be sad, depressed, lonely, or in need of a friend?

We're All in This Together

Session 1: You Going My Way?

Focal Passages: Psalm 1:1; Proverbs 12:26; 13:20; 18:24; 22:24-25
Life Destination: Preteens will discover the impact friends have on their lives and will learn to choose their friends wisely.
Memory Verse: Blessed is the man who does not walk in the counsel of the wicked or stand in the way of sinners or sit in the seat of mockers. *Psalm 1:1*

Session 2: A Friend Indeed!

Focal Passages: 1 Corinthians 13:4-7; John 15:12-13; Proverbs 15:1; 16:7,28-29; 17:17
Life Destination: Preteens will examine their own relationships in light of biblical principles.
Memory Verse: Do to others as you would have them do to you. *Luke 6:31*

Session 3: It's a Family Thing

Focal Passages: Proverbs 1:8; 10:1; 13:1; 15:5; 19:26; 20:20; 22:6; Ephesians 6:1-4
Life Destination: Preteens will discover God's plan for family relationships and will identify ways they can be loving family members themselves.
Memory Verse: Children, obey your parents in everything, for this pleases the Lord. *Colossians 3:20*

Unit Direction

Preteens will discover biblical truths about building and maintaining good relationships and will put those truths into practice with their family and friends.

Session 1
You Going My Way?

FOCAL PASSAGES:
Proverbs 12:26; 13:20;
18:24; 22:24-25;
Psalm 1:1

MEMORY VERSE:
Blessed is the man who
does not walk in the
counsel of the wicked
or stand in the way of
sinners or sit in the seat
of mockers. Psalm 1:1

LIFE DESTINATION:
Preteens will discover
the impact friends
have on their lives and
will learn to choose
their friends wisely.

How This Session Relates to Salvation

Preteens sometimes base their friendships on shallow and silly things. To be a true and valuable friend, preteens should have a personal relationship with the one true friend—Jesus Christ. Sixth graders need to know that their friendship choices should never compromise their personal relationship with Jesus.

Bible Study for Leaders

It didn't matter that Jill's shoes were a size-and-a-half too big. She was everything I wanted to be: mouthy, rebellious, well-dressed, and generous enough to loan me her platform sandals! I didn't even feel the blisters as I wobbled down the hall.

Preteens often experiment with friendships based on nothing more solid than a pair of cool shoes. But as the writers of Psalms and Proverbs teach us, friendships built on "fluff" can be fatal!

Results of Foolish Friendships

The writers of Proverbs were obviously aware that young people experiment with ill-advised friendships to prove their worldliness and independence. They got right to the point: fools choose fools for friends.

Well-meaning preteens (and adults) often rationalize that friendships with worldly, bad-tempered, carnal persons won't affect their lifestyles or their testimonies. However, each of today's focal Scriptures suggests that a person can easily be led astray (Proverbs 12:26), harmed (Proverbs 13:20), and influenced to behave like the immoral friend he associates with (Proverbs 22:24-25).

A caution as you teach: be ready to deal with the issue of cliques with your preteens. Some "well-churched" preteens go to great lengths to exclude non-Christian schoolmates and outsiders. In doing so, they appear petty and snobbish. Remind preteens that avoiding harmful friendships does not provide an excuse for them to be unfriendly.

Rewards of Wise Friendships

The wisdom writers painted vivid word pictures of the benefits of godly friendships. A person who avoids ungodly friends is "like a tree planted by streams of water ... whatever he does prospers" (Psalm 1:3). One who chooses friends cautiously is righteous (Proverbs 12:26) and who associates with the wise will become wise himself (Proverbs 13:20).

Preteens often treat friendships as trophies. A friend says her daughter's typical after-school chat begins like this: "Well, Mandy was the most popular today because Carissa decided to start hanging around her, and if Carissa hangs around her, then Alicia and Whitney will too. Mandy must have at least ten friends in her group!" Proverbs 18:24 helps us understand that collecting friends as status symbols is just as dangerous as associating with the "wrong crowd." True and godly friendships are rare and precious. Pray that your preteens will learn to value them.

DISCUSS AND DO

GET READY

• Get these items from the resource box: Poster 3, video, checkered flag.
• Gather: *Preteen Handbooks*, a 24-inch length of string for each preteen, several inflated balloons, a laundry basket.
• Secure a VCR and monitor.

GET SET

• Display Poster 3 on a focal wall.
• Arrange chairs around the edge of your classroom to leave space for active games.
• Scatter the inflated balloons on the floor. Set the laundry basket in the center of the room.
• Set up the VCR and monitor. Cue the video to the beginning of the third segment, "The Interview."

GET STARTED

1. Work with a friend. Hand each preteen a length of string. Instruct preteens to choose partners, then to tie their wrists together as illustrated in "Wrangle and Untangle!" on page 19 of the *Preteen Handbook*.

Call attention to Poster 3. Say, "You and your friend are in this together!" Challenge each pair to perform the following stunts without breaking or untying the strings:

• Do 20 jumping jacks.
• Take one another's shoes off and put them back on.
• Scratch one another's backs.
• Maneuver a balloon into the laundry basket using feet only.

After preteens have attempted each stunt, hold up the checkered flag. Say: "When the flag drops, untangle yourself from your partner without breaking or untying your strings." Drop the flag and enjoy the fun as preteens try to maneuver themselves apart. After a few minutes, reveal the simple trick to untangling the strings. (See second HINT, Step 1, for solution.)

2. Introduce today's Life Destination. Call for a volunteer to read the definition of friendship from "Factionary" on page 19 of the *Preteen Handbook*. Say: "Today, you'll discover that it can be extremely difficult to untangle yourself from an unwise friendship. Your best strategy is to be choosy about your friends before a friendship leads to trouble."

Play "The Interview." When the video concludes, ask: "What characteristics do you think Tiffany was looking for in her friends? Did the interviewers measure up to her standards? Why or why not?" *(They all wanted something from her.)* "How could Tiffany have been a better friend to Megan and Jessica?" *(She could have not opened the note. She could have talked to them about her feelings instead of just getting mad at them.)*

Say: "You may not choose your friends by conducting formal interviews—but today's Bible passages will help you understand the importance of choosing friends wisely!"

STEP 1

HINT

Boy/girl relationships are not highlighted in this session; however, this unit contains important truths that can be applied to opposite-sex friendships. If your students are mature enough, emphasize that the principles in Proverbs apply to all friendships.

STEP 1

HINT

How to "untangle" the "wrangle:"

1. Pass the loop of your rope through the loop tied around your friend's wrist.

2. Slide your loop over your friend's hand.

3. Pull your loop back through your friend's wrist loop. The ropes should now be separated.

HINT

As they discuss friendships, preteens may be tempted to gossip about specific acquaintances. Gently override their comments by saying, "Names don't matter right now. Our goal is to be alert to the kinds of friendships we want to avoid."

HINT

Answers to "Say What?"
1. cautious
2. suffers harm
3. learns his ways and is ensnared
4. may come to ruin

DIG
GET READY
• Get this item from the resource box: foam hand.
• Gather: Bibles, *Preteen Handbooks*, pencils, several self-sticking note pads.

GET STARTED
3. Discover what kind of friendships to avoid. Form three teams. (If possible, assign an adult leader to moderate each discussion). Instruct Team 1 to walk around the room as they read Psalm 1:1 together and to think of a present-day example of walking in the way of the wicked. Instruct Team 2 to stand as they read Psalm 1:1 and to name an example of standing in the way of sinners. Instruct Team 3 to sit as they read Psalm 1:1 and to give a present-day example of sitting in the seat of mockers. Guide them to "Factionary" on page 19 of the *Preteen Handbook* for the definition of "mocker."

Lead each team to share its observations with the large group. Say: "You probably know people who fit each of these categories." Guide each team to complete and discuss "They're on the Loose!" (*Preteen Handbook*, page 20).

4. Discover the pitfalls of dangerous friendships. Say: "The writers of Proverbs warned strongly against making friends with the kinds of people described in Psalm 1:1." Read aloud the definition of "fool" from "Factionary." Set the foam hand on the floor pointing to a specific corner of the room. Designate that area as the "pit." Guide each student to complete "Say What?" on page 20 of *Preteen Handbook*, then to move to the "pit" if she can identify a pitfall of choosing friends unwisely.

Lead preteens who have moved to the "pit" to share their answers. As preteens share, direct them back to their seats.

Enlist an adult leader to stand in the "pit." Give each preteen two or three sticky notes. Say: "Friends chosen unwisely can bring you down. Think about a habit or action that can destroy a friendship. Write it on a note and stick it to your leader."

5. Discover what kind of friendships to pursue. Enlist a preteen to read aloud Proverbs 18:24. Challenge preteens to define or describe a "friend who sticks closer than a brother." Emphasize that the Bible teaches that the quantity of friends a person has is much less important than the quality of friends a person has.

Enlist a second adult leader to stand just outside the "pit." Give each preteen two or three sticky notes. Guide students to write characteristics of true friends on the notes and stick them to the leader.

Stand between the two "stuck-up" teachers. Call attention the notes fastened to each one. Challenge each student to decide whether his actions bring his friends down or build his friends up.

DECIDE

GET READY

• Gather: blank notebook paper, pencils.

• Secure: a CD or cassette player and a contemporary Christian song about friendships to play during this segment.

• If available, bring a sample job application from your workplace.

GET STARTED

6. Develop criteria for choosing friends. State: "Your friendships matter to God." Give each preteen a blank sheet of paper and a pencil. Show the job application you brought. Invite preteens to design an application for a godly friend based on the positive and negative characteristics they found in Proverbs. Softly play the recording you brought as students work.

Invite preteens to name some of the qualifications they would consider "must-haves" in a friendship. Encourage others to name characteristics that would, in their opinion, immediately rule out a candidate for friendship.

7. Evaluate preteens' friendship choices. Lead preteens to flip their applications over and to list the names of several close friends on the back of the application. Say: "Take a few minutes to think how each of these friends might complete your application. Have you discovered that you have some friends who are bring-ing you down? What do you think God wants you to do about that friendship?" Assure students that this activity is absolutely private and that they do not have to share their thoughts or answers.

Before today's Bible study concludes, lead students to think about the godly way to treat friends who didn't meet the qualifications on their friendship applications. Use these questions as discussion starters: "Should you immediately quit talking to friends who bring you down? What happens when a group of Christian friends shuts out an outsider? Can you be a friend to an ungodly person without becoming ungodly yourself? How can you show friendship to a person who is rude, hot-tempered, or unwise?" Help preteens understand that choosing not to pursue a friendship with a person is not an excuse for being unfriendly or unkind.

Lead in a brief prayer asking God to help each preteen honor Him with their choice of friends. As students leave, direct them to remove one of the positive self-sticking messages from their leader, and to put the note on a mirror or locker to help them remember to choose godly friends.

HINT

You can vary the friendship application activity slightly by allowing students to trade and complete one another's applications, or by leading each student to complete his own application after it is prepared.

Session 2

A Friend Indeed!

FOCAL PASSAGES:
1 Corinthians 13:4-7;
John 15:12-13; Proverbs
15:1; 16:7,28-29; 17:17

MEMORY VERSE:
Do to others as you
would have them do
to you. Luke 6:31

LIFE DESTINATION:
Preteens will examine
their own relationships
in light of biblical
principles.

How This Session Relates to Salvation

The connection is clear: Jesus called us His friends, then proved it by dying for our sins. Christians should be willing to follow Jesus' example by showing sacrificial, unselfish love to their friends.

Bible Study for Leaders

Grab a piece of scratch paper (we'll wait while you go get it). Now: make two columns. Think of the sweet and selfless things your best friends have done for you over the years. Place an X in the first column for each incident you recall. In the second column, place an X for each sweet and selfless act you have performed for your friends over the same time period.

Perhaps your results were different—mine were embarrassingly lopsided. But, you know what? Our focal passages remind us that true friends don't care about the score!

A Tough Act to Follow

It was the eve of Jesus' death, and instead of wallowing in self-pity, He poured out His heart to His friends. In Jesus' "farewell address" to the disciples (John 14-16), He urged them to obey Him by loving one other with unselfish, big-hearted love. Less than 24 hours later, Jesus demonstrated His love for His friends by willingly laying down His life. Our willingness to extend Christlike friendship to others is a strong indicator of the condition of our friendship with Jesus (see John 15:12,14).

A Tough Kind of Love

Since the earliest days of literature, writers have tried to nail down the precise words to describe the "feeling" of love. As you read 1 Corinthians 13, notice that Paul doesn't discuss a feeling at all! Instead, he uses pedal-to-the-metal terminology to show how love acts, even under rough road conditions.

Two key terms that demonstrate love's resilience appear in 1 Corinthians 13:7. *Stego* is the original Greek word that is translated "always protects" or "beareth all things." It means to cover over something or to endure with patience. The second strong phrase, "always perseveres," translated from *hupomeno*, indicates that love bears much under pressure without breaking, a feat that could never be accomplished by weak and watery emotion!

A "Tough Cookie!"

Wise words in Proverbs also prove that a true friend is a "tough cookie!" Proverbs 15:1 indicates that a true friend exercises self-control and answers gently when provoked. He resists the temptation to jump into arguments and power struggles (Proverbs 16:28). He refuses to cause his friends to sin (Proverbs 16:29). He accepts his friends for who they are, and stands by them in times of crisis (Proverbs 17:17). Because his first priority is to please God, few people can find reasons to oppose him (Proverbs 16:7).

Christlike love is neither weak nor wimpy. Preteens who understand that principle can be powerful and valuable friends.

DISCUSS AND DO

GET READY
• Get these items from the resource box: the checkered flag, Poster 3.
• Gather: *Preteen Handbooks*, pencils.
• Make a copy of "How Do You Measure Up?" for every four to five preteens. (See "Stuff to Copy", page 48)
• Secure: several rulers, tape measures, and hand-held calculators.
• (Optional) Bring a CD or cassette player and a contemporary Christian recording about friendship.

GET SET
• Arrange your room to allow for active movement during this segment.

GET STARTED
1. Measure physical characteristics. Form teams of four to five preteens. Give each team measuring equipment, a calculator, and a copy of "How Do You Measure Up?" Direct preteens to measure themselves collectively as directed in the activity. If you brought an appropriate recording, play it as preteens "measure up."

Stop the activity by pausing the recording or dropping the checkered flag. Lead teams to report results, and determine the "champions" in each category.

2. Introduce today's Life Destination. Say: "You've had some fun measuring physical characteristics. We are going to use the rest of

the session to measure our 'friendship potential.'" Call attention to Poster 3. Ask: "What message does this cartoon convey about friendship?" *(Friends stick together even in tough and scary situations.)*

Give each student a *Preteen Handbook* and a pencil. Call attention to "A Friend Is ..." on page 21. Direct students to walk around the room and fill out each other's *Preteen Handbooks* with their own definitions of friendship. Continue to play music as students interact. Stop the music or drop the checkered flag to signal preteens to return to their seats. Encourage preteens to examine the definitions their friends wrote, choose their favorites, and share them with the group.

Lead a volunteer to locate and read Proverbs 17:17. Ask: "How does your favorite definition of friendship measure up to this verse?" Discuss.

Challenge preteens: "As you examine Bible verses about friendship today, think about how you measure up to the qualities they describe."

DIG

GET READY:
• Get these items from the resource box: foam hand, key.
• Gather: Bibles, *Preteen Handbooks*, pencils, markers, tape, two large sheets of paper, and a yardstick.
• Secure: two or three Bible dictionaries.

STEP 1

HINT
Painfully shy preteens may feel out of place standing head-to-head or toe-to-toe with classmates they don't know well. If this is the case, assign the shy preteen the job of "measurement recorder." The student can participate without getting uncomfortably "close and personal."

STEP 4

HINT

Form two teams by requiring preteens to line up numerically by telephone prefix, alphabetically by the second letter in their last names, or by shoe size. Then split the line in half. (This is a sneaky way to break up cliques or groups with "bad chemistry.")

STEP 4

HINT

Even among Christian preteens at Bible study, an outsider can feel lonely and conspicuous. If you observe a student standing on the sidelines, act as a stand-in friend during today's session. Plan to show Christlike friendship to that student (through a note, a treat, or an appropriate hug) this week.

GET SET:
• Tape the sheets of paper to a wall.
• Write the text of Luke 6:31 on the back of the yardstick with a permanent marker.

GET STARTED

3. Discover what friendship is not. Say: "Nowhere in the Bible will you find a concise definition of friendship. What you will find is a clear description of what a friend does or does not do." Let's start by examining the 'does nots.'" Lead preteens to pair up and complete "Break It Up!" on page 22 of their *Preteen Handbooks*. Monitor each pair's progress and encourage preteens to look up unfamiliar terms (*perverse, dissension, gossip, entice*) in "Factionary" on page 21 of the *Preteen Handbook* or in a Bible dictionary.

Challenge each pair to name a time when one of the actions described in Proverbs 16:28-29 destroyed or damaged their friendships.

4. Discover what friendship is. Form two teams, roughly equal in size, and direct each team to one of the sheets posted on the wall. Assign an adult leader to assist each team. Say: "You have already discovered what the Bible says a friend should never do. Now you will discover what the Bible says a real friend should *always* do."

Give Team 1 the foam hand and a marker. Assign students to complete "Super Glue" on page 22 of their *Preteen Handbooks*, then to draw a diagram of a godly friend as described in the verses. Preteens can draw a body outline with arrows pointing to specific parts. (*Sample captions: hands– "always ready to help" or mouth–"always speaks kindly."*) Instruct Team 1 to prepare a presentation about the diagram they created, using the foam hand as a pointer.

Give Team 2 the key, a marker, and a roll of tape. Lead preteens to read 1 Corinthians 13:4-7 and design a large poster that conveys the key characteristics of a loving friend. (If they wish, they can tape the key directly on the poster as part of the design.) Tell team members to be ready to point out key ideas from the poster to the large group.

TEAM LEADERS: As you talk through each activity with preteens, encourage them to name specific ways they can show patience, kindness, gentleness, and other biblical characteristics to their friends.

Allow students time to complete their projects, then lead each team to report.

5. Understand the Golden Rule. Using the yardstick as a pointer (conceal the memory verse side), point to the chart Team 1 prepared. Ask: "How many of you would like to have a friend with these qualities?" (Call for a show of hands.) Repeat the question while pointing to Team 2's poster.

Say: "A true friend concentrates on what he can give to a friendship, not what he can get from it." Flip over the yardstick and lead students to read Luke 6:31 aloud together. Challenge preteens to determine how following the Golden Rule can save a failing friendship or strengthen a healthy friendship.

DECIDE

GET READY

- Gather: card stock, red paper, tape, a craft knife.
- Make a copy of the insert and the "Friendometer" for each student. (See "Stuff to Copy" on page 48.)
- Write the following terms on individual slips of paper: *patient, kind, does not envy, does not boast, is not proud, is not rude, is not self-seeking, not easily angered, keeps no record of wrongs, does not delight in evil, protects, trusts, hopes, perseveres.*
- Secure: a wide rubber band (#64 size or wider) for each student and several extra-fine point markers.

GET STARTED

6. Examine friendship strengths and weaknesses.

Give each preteen a "Friendometer." Distribute the slips of paper you prepared to individual students. Direct each student to define the term in his own words when you call for a response. (Allow preteens time to formulate their definitions.)

Ask: "What kind of friend are you?" Direct preteens to listen to the definition of each friendship quality as it is shared and show where they rate on the "Friendometer" by inserting the red strip and moving the strip up or down. Suggest to preteens that this activity is private and that

they will keep their answers to themselves.

Read 1 Corinthians 13:4-7, stopping at the word "patient." Call for the pre-enlisted student to stand, define the term, then guide students to use the "Friendometer" to measure their patience level. Read the next phrase and follow the same procedure. Continue, pausing after each key phrase for definitions and evaluation.

7. Develop a strategy for becoming a better friend.

Give each preteen a wide rubber band and a marker. Say: "Think about the friendship categories in which you rated yourself below medium. Write them on the rubber band. Wear the rubber band around your wrist."

Explain that students can use the rubber bands as a reminder during the week to come. Each time they catch themselves being impatient, or being tempted to gossip, they should snap themselves lightly with the rubber band. The sting will interrupt the thought or action, and they can stop and think about being a better friend. (For fun, allow students to make a "practice snap.")

8. Pray together.
Form small groups and assign an adult leader to each group. Instruct each group leader to pray for the students by name, asking God to make them loving and unselfish friends.

STEP 7

HINT
Remind preteens that true friends do not "snap" each other with rubber bands. The bands are to be snapped only by the persons wearing them.

Session 3

It's a Family Thing

FOCAL PASSAGES:
Proverbs 1:8; 10:1; 13:1; 15:5; 19:26; 20:20; 22:6; Ephesians 6:1-4

MEMORY VERSE:
Children obey your parents in everything, for this pleases the Lord. Colossians 3:20

LIFE DESTINATION:
Preteens will discover God's plan for family relationships and will identify ways they can be loving family members themselves.

How This Session Relates to Salvation

"Respect my father?" Some of your preteens come from difficult family circumstances and may not understand how or why they should honor non-Christian parents. This week, you can help students understand that their respect and gentleness to all family members can be a powerful witness to their own relationship with the Heavenly Father.

Bible Study for Leaders

My parents' IQ increased dramatically when I left home, doubled when I got married, and tripled when I had a child of my own! As a flighty preteen, I had no clue that someday I'd be calling them for advice on everything from cleaning up an exploded Thanksgiving turkey to coaxing a five-year-old to draw with any other color besides orange.

Because He Said So!

Nearly all parents, when pushed to the disciplinary limit, have occasionally responded to a whining "Why?" with, "Because I said so!" The thought is that if Mom said it, that's it! In the matter of respect for parents, God said so, and that is it. However, God *didn't* command children to "honor ... just because." He promised that children who treat their parents with gentleness, respect, and unselfishness would prosper. (See Ephesians 6:2-3; Deuteronomy 5:16.)

According to the Book of Proverbs, obedience is only one phase of honoring one's parents. Honor also involves:
• Listening to a parent's instructions and warnings (1:8; 13:1).
• Bringing joy to a parent (10:1).
• Accepting discipline gracefully (15:5).
• Respecting parents' property and financial resources (19:26).
• Speaking pleasantly to and about parents (20:20).

It Goes Both Ways

After a particularly challenging disciplinary session with our son, he said bluntly, "Mom, this disciplining thing is a puzzle you and Dad will never figure out!" He's closer to the truth than he knows! The only thing I have figured out is that parents who refuse to treat their children with respect are just as rebellious in God's sight as children who refuse to obey.

Ephesians 6:4 contains two powerful parenting principles. First, parents are not to exasperate or provoke their children. Secondly, parents are to lovingly teach their children to obey God's Word through example and firm, gentle discipline.

Bringing up children "in the training and instruction of the Lord" can be frustrating, but the result described in Proverbs 22:6 is exhilarating. It is true that godly parents sometimes have wayward children, it is also true that godly, careful parenting can produce reverent, respectful, responsible children. The key to healthy relationships at home is mutual respect—it's a family thing!

DISCUSS AND DO

GET READY

• Get these items from the resource box: video, checkered flag, Poster 3.

• Gather: *Preteen Handbooks*, pencils, several packs of three-by-five-inch cards or flash cards, a slip of paper and an envelope for each preteen.

• Write the following on three-fourths of the slips of paper: "Carefully and *silently* build a house of cards." Write the following on one-fourth of the slips of paper: "Without being detected by your teammates, make the card house fall." Seal each slip inside an envelope. Secretly mark the "sabotage" directions for your convenience.

• Secure a VCR and monitor.

GET SET

• Arrange chairs around several small work tables. Place a stack of cards on each table.

• Set up the VCR and monitor. Cue the video to the beginning of the fourth segment, "Let's Talk about It."

GET STARTED

1. Participate in an activity that requires cooperation.

As preteens arrive, give each one a sealed envelope and route her to a table. Signal "no talking" with your hand and guide students to begin constructing card houses at each table. (Plant a reliable student with "tear-down" orders at each table.) Say: "If your team successfully completes a house using every card in the stack, come and claim the checkered flag."

Continue to encourage silence as the teams concentrate and work to create a successful card house. (If your pre-enlisted students do their jobs properly, no team should complete their house.)

Call time after a few frustrated attempts. Reveal the secret orders assigned to one student at each table.

Ask: "Is there a connection between the card house game and your own family relationships? If so, what?" *(Possible responses: families work together to build a home; it only takes one person to tear the home apart.)* Call attention to Poster 3. Lead preteens to determine that God expects mutual respect and cooperation from all family members. Say: "If any family member fails to support the others, the family is less than God intends it to be."

2. Discuss what tears down a family.

Distribute *Preteen Handbooks*. Tell preteens to examine the definition of "family" in the "Factionary" on page 23. Say: "Let's think about some things that tear down those important family relationships." Direct students to read "How Not to Be a Family Member," on page 23 of the *Preteen Handbook*. Instruct preteens to write their own comments in the empty cartoon balloons. Invite volunteers to share their responses. Ask: "Is there a common link that connects these responses?" *(Lack of respect for family members.)*

STEP 1

HINT

Depending on the maturity of your students, you may wish to assign an adult leader to each work table to serve as the "ringer" who discreetly causes the card houses to collapse.

3. Watch a video. Play "Let's Talk about It." Ask: "What does it mean to 'put yourself in another person's shoes'?" *(You think about how that person might feel; you see things from their point of view.)* "How can that be helpful in a family situation?" *(You would be more understanding.)* "Why is important to take the time to discuss your feelings instead of simply reacting?" *(It is a way to show respect.)*

Say: "God's plan for families requires children to honor their parents and parents to respect their children."

DIG

GET READY
• Get the following item from the resource box: foam hand.
• Gather: Bibles, *Preteen Handbooks,* pencils, scissors, construction paper, markers, tape, one piece of individually wraped candy for each preteen.
• Make a three-link paper chain. Label the first link "God," the second link "Parent," and the third link "Child."

GET SET
• Place tape, scissors, markers, and construction paper on each table.
• Assign an adult leader to work with each small group.

GET STARTED
4. Discover God's plan for families. Say: "You know that part of God's plan for families is for children to obey their parents—and we'll talk about that in a few minutes. But first, let's think about the

requirements and responsibilities God has given your parents."

Instruct teams at each table to complete "It Goes Both Ways" on page 24 of *Preteen Handbook,* then to use the supplies on the table to create a quick and simple paper sculpture that illustrates God's plan for families.

When preteens have completed their assignment, invite a spokesperson from each team to describe what its sculpture represents.

Show your paper chain. Point with the foam hand to the corresponding links as you explain: "Here's my sculpture. According to God's Word, there's a definite chain of command in a family. As a child, I have to answer to my parents, but my parents have to answer to God. Or to think about it differently, God gives my parents authority to have authority over me."

5. Discover the rewards of honoring parents. Say: "We should be willing to obey and honor our parents just because God says so, but the Bible names many other rewards of honoring parents. Let's dig to discover some of those rewards." Instruct teams of preteens to complete "Just Because" on page 24 in the *Preteen Handbook.*

GROUP LEADERS: As preteens work, lead them to identify reasons they sometimes have difficulty respecting their parents. Point out the definition of "discipline" in the "Factionary" on page 23 of the *Preteen Handbook* and challenge preteens to identify times when their parents' discipline helped them

STEP 5

HINT
More rewards of graciously accepting discipline can be found in Hebrews 12:11.

avoid mistakes or helped them become a wiser person.

When students have completed their small group work, say: "I have a gift for students who can stand and name a benefit of respecting and honoring their parents." Give or toss a piece of candy to each student who responds correctly.

DECIDE

GET READY

- Get these items from the resource box: Poster 4, foam hand, key.
- Gather: scissors, markers, a dictionary.
- Secure: small picture frames with loop hangers, and metal looseleaf rings (one each per student). If the frames do not have a backing that can be reversed and written on, cut small inserts from poster board.

GET SET

- Attach Poster 4 to the focal wall.
- Place picture frame supplies on each table.
- Assign an adult leader to work with each small group.

GET STARTED

6. Discover and define keys to loving family relationships. Say: "So far, you have discovered that God requires respect from all family members. Now, let's think about some specific attitudes and actions that will help us build up our families."

Instruct preteens to read James 3:17. Tell students that each of the characteristics mentioned in the Scripture is hidden some-where in Poster 4. Direct students to begin their search by looking for the word "pure." Instruct the student who finds the word first to put on the foam hand, point to the word on the poster, and explain how being pure contributes to the strength of a family. Continue in the same way until all the following words are found and defined: *pure, peace-loving, considerate, submissive, full of mercy, impartial, sincere.* If students are "stumped" defining any term, direct them to find the term in the dictionary and to try again. Be sure to emphasize that these qualities apply to sibling relationships as well as parent-child relationships.

7. Create a reminder. Review each of the terms hidden in the poster. Point with the key to the poster with the key and say: "One of these characteristics may be the key to improving relationships in your family." Direct students to select a key word, print it creatively on the frame insert, and assemble a key chain by threading the ring through the top loop of the frame.

GROUP LEADERS: Guide each preteen to name a specific action he will take this week to reflect the characteristic written on his key chain.

While still assembled in small groups, pray for each student by name, asking God to help the student be a loving and respectful family member.

STEP 6

HINT
Preteens experiencing difficult family circumstances may have little reason to respect their parents. Help those students recognize the healing, helpful effect showing honor can have on a less-than-ideal family situation.

STEP 7

HINT
Simple key chains can also be made with squares of mat board. Punch a hole in the corner of the mat board, and loop a notebook ring through the hole.

 Stuff to Copy

For use in Session 2, Step 1.
Make a copy of this sheet for each team of students.

How Do You Measure Up?

Find a group of friends. Measure your:

Grin Potential (the total length of each of your combined smiles at the widest point)

_____

Hug Factor (the length of the entire group standing with arms outstretched)

_____

Handshake Quotient (the height of all your right hands stacked on a table)

_____

Head Exponent (the number of inches around all your heads when you stand back-to-back in a circle)

_____

Foot Multiplier (the total length of the group's feet when placed heel-to-toe)

_____

Pinky Power (the total length of all your pinky fingers)

_____

For use in Session 2, Step 6. Make a copy for each preteen on card stock.

Make a copy on red paper and cut one for each preteen.

Love is patient, love is kind. It does not envy, it does not boast, it is not proud. It is not rude, it is not self-seeking, it is not easily angered, it keeps no record of wrongs. Love does not delight in evil but rejoices with the truth. It always protects, always trusts, always hopes, always perserveres.

1Corinthians 13:4-7

FRIENDOMETER

— MOST EXCELLENT!
—
— SUPERB
—
— PRETTY GOOD
—
— BETTER THAN AVERAGE
—
— MEDIUM
—
— LESS THAN AVEREGE
—
— NOT TOO GREAT
—
— UH-OH
—
— YOU GOTTA BE KIDDING!

Cut Slit

48

UNIT 4

From the Inside Out

Session 1: Just Forget about It

Focal Passages: Acts 6:8-15; 7:51-60
Life Destination: Preteens will follow Stephen's example of forgiveness.
Memory Verse: Bear with each other and forgive whatever grievances you may have against one another. Forgive as the Lord forgave you. *Colossians 3:13*

Session 2: You Go First

Focal Passages: Ruth 1:8-18; 2:1-23
Life Destination: Preteens will show kindness and compassion to those around them as they seek to follow Ruth's example.
Memory Verse: Be kind and compassionate to one another, forgiving each other, just as in Christ God forgave you. *Ephesians 4:32*

Session 3: I'll Wait

Focal Passages: 1 Samuel 16:14-23; 17:10-22,32-37,48-50; 18:5; 2 Samuel 2:1-4; 5:1-4
Life Destination: Preteens will discover what it means to "wait upon the Lord" as they determine areas of impatience in their own lives.
Memory Verse: Wait for the LORD; be strong and take heart and wait for the LORD. *Psalm 27:14*

Unit Direction

Preteens will examine the following character traits through the lives of Bible people who exhibited them:
• Forgiveness—Stephen
• Kindness—Ruth
• Long-suffering—David
  Preteens will be able to model these examples in their own lives as they seek to develop these traits.

Session 1
Just Forget about It

FOCAL PASSAGES:
Acts 6:8-15; 7:51-60

MEMORY VERSE:
Bear with each other and forgive whatever grievances you may have against one another. Forgive as the Lord forgave you. Colossians 3:13

LIFE DESTINATION:
Preteens will follow Stephen's example of forgiveness.

How This Session Relates to Salvation

Understanding what true forgiveness means is an important part of understanding and accepting God's forgiveness for our sins. His example of forgiveness shows us how to forgive others.

Bible Study for Leaders

Stephen, a man with a solid spiritual reputation, had been chosen by his peers to serve in the early church. His ministry and his dedication to God became widely known among the people. The people witnessed the power of God through the supernatural wonders that Stephen performed.

The leaders of the various synagogues soon began to feel threatened. They could not match Stephen's wisdom in oral debates, so great was the Spirit of God in Stephen. False witnesses appeared before the Sanhedrin and claimed they had heard Stephen speak blasphemy.

As the intense glares of the Sanhedrin bore down on Stephen, the Bible says his face was like that of an angel. When it was Stephen's turn to speak, he didn't mince words. He told the court in no uncertain terms that they were more guilty than those they tried to condemn. He accused them of resisting the Holy Spirit and of killing the Righteous One of God. This made the Sanhedrin so mad their teeth were grinding.

But Stephen, filled with the Spirit, looked up and saw Jesus standing at the right hand of God. In awe, Stephen described the scene. The mob became even more incensed and grabbed Stephen, carried him outside the city gates, and began to stone him.

With his last breath Stephen asked Jesus to receive his spirit and begged for the forgiveness of his persecutors.

The Main Character

We only are given snippets of Stephen's life story. But all the days of his life, all the conversations he had, all the actions others observed, must have formed the qualifications for that one sentence in Acts 6:5 "a man full of faith and of the Holy Spirit." In Acts 6:8, we are told that Stephen was a man full of God's grace and power!

What great things a man like this might have accomplished had he lived a few more years! Yet, it is this one moment that touches our lives even now. Stephen gave us a picture of forgiveness that we will never forget.

As Stephen's body began to crumble under the onslaught of hurling rocks, his faith in God gave him peace. The grace of God gave him a spirit of forgiveness for those whose souls were in even greater danger than his body.

The Preteen Connection

Preteens can discover that, no matter how unfair or cruel circumstances may seem, God's grace can help us have a forgiving spirit. Forgiveness releases us from energy wasted on negative feelings and offers an example to those around us of God's power to forgive.

DISCUSS AND DO

GET READY

• Get these items from the resource box: Poster 5, checkered flag.

• Gather: a sheet of poster board, markers, tape, a three-feet-by-six-feet strip of paper, a disposable cup, *Preteen Handbooks.*

• Prepare the following items: fill an empty two-liter soda bottle with water and secure the cap, fill a popcorn tin with foam packing material, select a "boring" info tape and place it in the jacket of a current popular video.

• Secure: VCR and monitor, table for display.

• On the large strip of paper, draw irregularly shaped ovals to resemble stones in a stone wall. Each stone should be large enough for preteens to write phrases inside.

• Write "FORGIVE" vertically on the poster board.

GET SET

• Set up VCR and monitor.

• Arrange the three items you prepared on a display table beside the VCR.

• Fan-fold Poster 5 along the dotted lines so that only the top third (the rock) shows.

• Attach the "stone wall" to a focal wall.

GET STARTED

1. Discover what's on the inside. Welcome preteens as they arrive. Direct them to find a comfortable spot where they can see easily see the monitor. Call attention to the display you have set up. Ask: "Can anyone guess what I have planned today?"

Begin by opening the soda bottle. Invite someone to sample a cup to see if it is "flat." The volunteer will discover that it is only water.

Invite another volunteer to open the popcorn tin. Preteens will begin to get the idea that things are not what they appear to be.

Adopt an "oh, well" approach and explain that at least you have the movie. Pop in the video and watch it for a minute or two.

Ask: "Is there something we can learn from what just happened here?" *(Regardless of what we see on the outside, it is what's inside that counts.)* Call attention to Poster 5. Say: "Let look at this another way. An ordinary rock (unfold poster and attach it to the wall) can be beautiful inside."

Say: "During this unit we will be looking at three individuals who had remarkable characteristics. They didn't have these characteristics because they were different from you or me. They had them because of a strength they had on the inside that came from God."

2. Determine what it means to forgive. Attach the poster on which you have written "FORGIVE" to a focal wall. Encourage preteens to help you understand what it means to forgive by naming some things that have to do with forgiveness. Write any words or phrases that fit into the acrostic in the appropriate place. Write any other words or phrases around the border of the poster.

Direct preteens to read the

STEP 1

HINT

For greater effect, use a green soft drink bottle to disguise the contents of the bottle. Place a strip of tape around the lid of the popcorn tin so that it appears unopened. Decorate the display table with a table cloth, cups, napkins, and a centerpiece.

STEP 2

HINT

Words and phrases that can be used to complete the acrostic might include:

Forget

l**O**ve

t**R**ust

Good for you

gI**V**e another chance

no re**V**enge

no grudg**E**

STEP 4

HINT

Practice reading the article aloud so that it seems to come from the newspaper. Preteens will get caught up in the drama of the event before they get the opportunity to "tune out" a familiar Bible story.

STEP 5

HINT

Drawing a snack or treat out of a bag is a good way help students form teams. If you don't have chips, consider using candy that is available in three different colors, or three different flavors of gum.

definition of "forgive" in the "Factionary" on page 25 of the *Preteen Handbook*. Add any additional comments to the poster.

3. Discuss how difficult it can be to forgive. Show preteens the "stone wall" you have prepared. Invite each preteen to write at least one thing that is difficult to forgive one of the stones on the "wall." After several minutes, wave the checkered flag to signal that time is up.

Invite volunteers to share some of the things written on the wall. Acknowledge that some things are harder to forgive than others.

DIG

GET READY
• Gather: Bibles, a large clean trash bag, tape, pencils, *Preteen Handbooks*, current news magazines and newspapers.
• Secure: a snack-size bag of chips for each preteen. You will need equal numbers of three different kinds of chips.

GET SET
• Tape a copy of the news story from Step 4 inside a newspaper so that it appears to be a part of the paper.
• Place the bags of chips in the large trash bag.
• Make three or four copies of "Little Wang and Liang." (See "Stuff to Copy," page 62.)

GET STARTED
4. Share Stephen's story. Tell preteens that you would like to get their reaction to a story that you read recently.

Open the newspaper and read the following account:

Violence continued in Jerusalem as an angry mob killed a local citizen just outside the city. Witnesses claim the man had been helping a great number of people who were sick and in need. Unidentified sources report that religious officials, who were offended by this man's methods and beliefs, paid witnesses to bring charges against him.

Incited by the religious leaders, an angry mob carried the man outside the city and stoned him to death. Witnesses claim the man showed neither anger nor hostility toward his tormentors. In fact, he was heard praying for the forgiveness of those who were throwing the stones.

Invite volunteers to share the feelings they had as you read the story. Explain that while the "cover" was misleading (the story wasn't from last week's newspaper) the story inside was true. The man's name was Stephen and his story is in the Book of Acts.

5. Dig a little deeper. Form three teams by directing each preteen to reach into the trash bag and pull out a bag of chips. Preteens with matching chips will form a team. Assign an adult leader to each team. Give these directions:

TEAM LEADER 1: Guide your team to research Stephen by reading the first two entries in "Factionary" on page 25 of the *Preteen Handbook* and by completing "Who Is He, Anyway?" on page 26. (See first HINT, Step 5, for answers.)

TEAM LEADER 2: Guide your team to learn about "Little Wang and Liang" from the handout. Complete "It Still Happens" on page 25 of the *Preteen Handbook*.

TEAM LEADER 3: Guide your team look through the newspapers and magazine provided to find current stories of people who have experienced unfair circumstances. Complete "Even in My World" on page 26 of the *Preteen Handbook*.

After ten minutes, call for reports from each team. Instruct preteens to fill in the answers to each section in their *Preteen Handbook* as each team shares.

DECIDE

GET READY

• Get this item from the resource box: key.

• Gather: a large shoe box, aluminum foil, several rolls of transparent tape, rubber bands, a piece of construction paper, markers, pens, paper, a self-closing snack bag for each preteen, self-stick labels.

• Secure: a paper shredder.

• Cut one copy of today's memory verse (Col. 3:13) from page 33 of the *Preteen Handbook* for each preteen.

• Cover the shoe box with aluminum foil. (Cover the lid separately so that the box can be opened.) Attach the key to the top of the box with rubber bands.

• Write today's memory verse on construction paper and place it in the "key" box.

GET STARTED

6. Discover the key to forgiveness. Call attention to the "key box." Say: "Each week during this unit we will try to discover the "key" to a character trait God wants us to develop." Open the box, take out the memory verse, and read it aloud together. Explain that today's verse can help us find this week's key.

Ask: "Who is hurt the most when we fail to forgive?" *(We are.)* "Why should we forgive?" *(God has forgiven us.)*

Say: "When God asks us to do something that seems impossible—like forgiving someone who has hurt us very much—He gives us the strength and power we need to obey Him."

7. Forgive and forget. Give each preteen a pen and a piece of paper. Instruct preteens to list things that are hard for them to forgive.

Gather with preteens around the paper shredder. Direct students, one at a time, to shred their paper and put the shreds in a self-closing snack bag. Give each preteen a memory verse card. Instruct preteens to tape the verse to their bag of shredded paper.

Say: "Keep this 'shredded evidence' as a reminder that when God forgives our sins, He also forgets them. When someone hurts us, we can depend on God to help us forgive that person." Close with prayer.

HINT

Answers to "Who Is He, Anyway?"

1. faith, full of the Holy Spirit
2. blasphemy
3. False witnesses testified against him.
4. The members of the Sanhedrin were blaspheming God: they received the law but did not obey it.
5. stoning
6. "Lord, do not hold this sin against them."
7. Saul

HINT for Team Leader #3

Consider downloading articles from the Internet about incidents that are unfair or unjust. If you have difficulty finding appropriate material, share a time in your own life when it was difficult to forgive someone.

Session 2

You Go First

FOCAL PASSAGES:
Ruth 1:8-18; 2:1-23

MEMORY VERSE:
Be kind and compassionate to one another, forgiving each other, just as in Christ God forgave you.
Ephesians 4:32

LIFE DESTINATION:
Preteens will show kindness and compassion to those around them as they seek to follow Ruth's example.

How This Session Relates to Salvation

While further aspects of Ruth's story relate more directly to understanding God's plan of salvation, this part of her story lays the foundation. The example of faith Naomi set before her daughters-in-law encouraged Ruth to want to follow the one true God.

Bible Study for Leaders

Due to a famine in the land of Canaan, Naomi and her husband and two sons had moved into Moab to find food. While there, her sons met and married Moabite women, Ruth and Orpah. Before any children were born to the young couples, Naomi's husband and her two sons died. Naomi decided to return home to Bethlehem.

While both daughters-in-law pleaded to go with her, Naomi succeeded in convincing Orpah to return to her family. Ruth, however, could not be persuaded and continued on with her mother-in-law.

Naomi and Ruth arrived in Bethlehem just as the barley harvest was beginning. According to Israelite law, the poor could pick up grain dropped by the harvesters. (See Deut. 24:19.) Ruth set to work. While she worked diligently to provide for the needs of her mother-in-law and herself, she was noticed by the owner of the land, Boaz.

Boaz was impressed by the young woman and took steps to insure her safety, her comfort, and her success in gleaning the fields.

When Ruth shared the story with Naomi, Naomi recognized God's hand in all that had happened. She knew God was blessing Ruth for her kindness and faithfulness.

The Main Character

Why did Orpah go home and Ruth stay with her mother-in-law? I have heard many preachers and teachers praise one and put down the other. The truth is, the Bible does not say. It simply tells us what happened. However, a few observations can be "gleaned" from the passage. Both girls had been kind to Naomi. Both girls wanted to stay with Naomi and tried to convince her to let them go with her. Both girls were moved to tears and cared about Naomi (Ruth 1:8-14).

The difference may be in Ruth's speech to Naomi "Your God will be my God" (1:16) and her vow "May the Lord deal with me" (1:17). Ruth had embraced the faith of Naomi's family. She had turned away from the Moabite gods worshipped by her people. Ruth's faith gave her a heartfelt kindness strong enough to enable her to leave behind all she knew to stay with her widowed mother-in-law.

The Preteen Connection

It is easier to be kind and compassionate to others when it is convenient or when it does not require much of a personal sacrifice. However, there is a degree of kindness that we can express that requires a conscious decision. It requires strength and determination often beyond our own abilities. It requires the strength and power of God's Holy Spirit in our lives.

DISCUSS AND DO

GET READY

• Get this item from the resource box: video.

• Gather: freshly sharpened pencils, *Preteen Handbooks,* markers, large sheet of paper.

• Secure: beverage, cups, cookies, napkins, VCR and monitor.

• Preview the fifth video segment "Random Acts of Kindness." Make note of the various acts of kindness and the possible motives behind them.

GET SET

• Set up VCR and monitor. Cue the video to the beginning of "Random Acts of Kindness."

• Make a copy of the "Person Outline" for each preteen. (See "Stuff to Copy," page 62.)

GET STARTED

1. Experience kindness. During the first few moments as preteens arrive, invite all adult leaders to help you greet the students with exaggerated acts of kindness. (See HINT, Step 1, for examples.)

As preteens are seated, give each one a paper person. Make a big deal out of making sure it is a good copy with no wrinkles or tears. Pass around a plate of cookies and offer each preteen something to drink.

Ask: "Who can guess what we will be discussing today?" *(Kindness.)* Direct preteens to find "Factionary" on page 27 in their *Preteen Handbooks.*

Read together the definition of "kindness."

Ask: "Did the adult leaders illustrate genuine kindness to you this morning? Why or why not?"

2. Watch a video. Invite preteens to watch a video segment to see if they can identify some genuine acts of kindness. Play "Random Acts of Kindness."

After the video segment, encourage preteens to name some acts of kindness they observed in the video. List observations on a large sheet of paper.

Explain that motivation is what determines whether an act of kindness is genuine or selfish. (A act of "kindness" can be selfish if the motivation is to gain something for oneself.)

Look at the actions listed on the paper. Challenge preteens to identify actions that may not have been genuine kindness. Draw a line through those items. Draw a star by those actions that seemed genuine.

Instruct preteens to list on the "Person Outlines" some things they believe are elements of "being kind." When preteens finish writing, direct them to turn their "people" face down until later.

DIG

GET READY

• Gather: Bibles, one three-by-five-inch card for each preteen, a large sheet of paper, marker, tape, pencils, paper.

• Prepare: On half the cards draw a picture

STEP 1

HINT

Exaggerated acts of kindness might include:

• Using sticky-sweet baby voices when greeting them.

• Dusting off their chairs.

• Offering freshly sharpened pencils.

• Asking if they are comfortable. Are they too hot or too cold?

• Opening preteens' Bibles to the Book of Ruth.

• Offering more refreshments.

STEP 2

HINT

During the course of this session, help preteens to understand the difference between true kindness and just being nice to make an impression or to get something in return.

of a stalk of wheat or write the word "wheat." On the remaining cards draw a picture of a knapsack or write the word "knapsack."

GET SET
• Divide Bibles, paper, and pencils between two different locations in the room.
• Attach the large sheet of paper to the focal wall.

GET STARTED
3. Meet Ruth. Say: "Today we will be taking a look at Ruth. Ruth can help us understand what God wants when He asks us to show kindness. True kindness requires a greater effort than just 'being nice.' Being kind often involves choosing to act in a certain way regardless of the obstacles and without obvious rewards."

Direct preteen to draw from the pile of index cards you have prepared. (You may hold them out in a fan shape so that students may draw from anywhere in the stack.) Those who draw a picture of a knapsack will form Team 1. Those who draw a picture of wheat will form Team 2.
TEAM 1 LEADER: Lead your team to do the following:
• Read Ruth 1:8-18.
• Complete "Kinds of Kindness" on page 27 of the *Preteen Handbook*.
• Create a short drama illustrating the assigned passage. Use as many "kinds of kindness" from your list as possible in your presentation.
TEAM 2 LEADER: Lead your team to do the following:
• Read Ruth 2:1-23.
• Complete "Kinds of Kindness" on page 27 of the *Preteen Handbook*.

• Create a short drama illustrating the assigned passage. Use as many "kinds of kindness" from your list as possible in your presentation.

After about 10 minutes, call teams back together. Invite Team 1 to present its drama while Team 2 lists the kinds of kindness they recgonise in the presentation. Instruct Team 1 to do the same when Team 2 presents its drama.

After both groups have shared their presentations, call for volunteers from each team to name the "kinds of kindness" portrayed in the dramas. Write responses on a large sheet of paper.

DECIDE
GET READY
• Get this item from the resource box: Poster 5.
• Gather: Bibles, *Preteen Handbooks*, pencils, large sheet of construction paper, marker.
• Secure: a small award for each preteen (small gold-wrapped chocolate coin, small plastic trophy, a blue ribbon, etc.)
• Plan to reuse the "key box" from last week's session (See "GET READY" on page 53.)
• On the piece of construction paper write: "You have been nominated to receive a kindness award. Judges will be following you around all week. What will you do?" Roll up the paper and place it in the "key box."

GET STARTED
4. Discover the source of our strength. Ask: "Based on

HINT
When students perform story-related drama, provide Bible time costumes or props. Even an industrial size garbage bag with holes for the head and arms can be a costume when belted at the waist.

what we have discovered today, how has your definition of kindness changed from when you first arrived?"

Ask: "Based on last week's study of Stephen, what must we include with kindness?" *(Forgiveness.)* Instruct preteens to complete "Heart Matters" on page 28 of the *Preteen Handbook.*

Ask: "Where do we get the power to be kind even when it is most difficult?" *(From God.)* Remind preteens that even kindness on the "easiest" level is more effective when we do it with God's love.

Call attention to Poster 5. Say: "When God is in our lives, we have the strength and the beauty on the inside to do what He wants us to do on the outside."

5. Learn the memory verse. Direct preteens to locate the memory verse (Eph. 4:32) in their Bibles. Call for volunteers to read the verse aloud several times. Challenge preteens to say the verse without looking at their Bibles.

Direct preteens to look at the kindness characteristics they listed earlier on their "paper person." Allow time for preteens to add or change anything on their list.

Ask: "Is there someone you can think of to whom you need to be kind this week?" Instruct preteens to write that person's initials on their paper. Encourage preteens to copy today's memory verse on the back of their "person" as a reminder to show God's kindness to those around them.

6. Discover the key to kindness. Say: "This week's key to this characteristic—kindness—is in the form of a challenge." Open the "key box" and read the challenge: "You have been nominated to receive a kindness award. Judges will be following you around all week. What will you do?"

Guide the discussion as preteens suggest things they can do this week to show kindness. Remind preteens that even though human judges may not be following us around, God is always with us and He knows not only what we do, but why we do it.

7. Close in prayer. Invite preteens to bow their heads and close their eyes as you direct them in a silent prayer. Give these directions: "First, thank God for His examples of kindness both in the Bible and in the people around you. Next, ask God to show you opportunities to show the kindness He expects from you."

Before preteens leave, give each one a "mini-award." Explain that you know they all have "moments of kindness." Challenge preteens to keep their "mini-awards" as a way of remembering to be extra-sensitive to "kindness opportunities" and to depend on God's power to help them show His kindness.

STEP 6

HINT

Help preteens clairify what is and what is not a genuine act of kindness by reminding them that genuine kindness comes from a genuine concern for another person. Genuine kindness usually takes extra time and effort and often demands a sacrifice on our part.

Session 3

I'll Wait

FOCAL PASSAGES:
1 Samuel 16:14-23;
17:10-22,32-37,48-50;
18:5; 2 Samuel 2:1-4;
5:1-5

MEMORY VERSE:
Wait for the LORD; be strong and take heart and wait for the LORD. Psalm 27:14

LIFE DESTINATION:
Preteens will discover what it means to "wait upon the Lord" as they determine areas of impatience in their own lives.

How This Session Relates to Salvation

Part of realizing that God has a plan for each of us is realizing that the most important part of His plan is for us to come to know His Son as our personal Savior and Lord.

Bible Study for Leaders

When David was a young boy, God sent Samuel to anoint this sheep-herding youngest son of Jesse as the next king of Israel! (1 Samuel 16:11-13) However, a great deal of time would pass before this small shepherd boy would actually become the king of a nation.

Saul, the first king of Israel, failed to follow God as he should. He suffered mental disturbances brought on by an evil spirit. His only source of comfort during those difficult times was the sweet sound of a harp. And who do you suppose was brought in to play the harp? David. David was able to see first-hand the duties of a king. David was also given the position of the king's armor-bearer which provided him with valuable military training.

David alternated his time serving Saul with tending the sheep back home. Sheep require constant attention. The skills David learned in his various jobs would serve him well when he began looking after the welfare of an entire nation.

David was 30 years old before he became king over Judah. David followed God's leadership and chose Hebron for his headquarters.

Hebron was the largest city in Judah; it was secure against attack; and it was located near the center of the Judah territory where many key trade routes joined.

More than seven years later, the elders of the northern tribes of Israel came to David and asked him to be their king as well.

David then moved to Jerusalem where, for the next 33 years, he reigned over the united kingdom.

The Main Character

Even though David knew God had great plans for him, he never refused a task. He did everything from tending sheep to cleaning armor. An active, observant young man, David probably wondered when God would make him king! But David was patient, and he did each thing God sent his way to the best of his ability.

David was 30 years old when he finally became king. The promise was fulfilled when God decided David was ready.

The Preteen Connection

Sixth graders may feel like they are stranded in the "wait" zone. On the threshold of teenage independence, they are too old for some things and too young for others.

Preteens need to learn that waiting on God does not mean doing nothing, but means accepting things God sends their way as the next step in the best plan He has for their lives.

DISCUSS AND DO
GET READY
• Get this item from the resource box: Poster 6.
• Gather: a large sheet of paper, markers, masking tape, clear Contact® Paper.
• Cover Poster 6 with clear Contact Paper or laminate.
• Make one copy of the "Thought Balloon" on page 62 ("Stuff to Copy") for each preteen.

GET SET
• Assign adult leaders a job to be "finishing" as preteens arrive. *(Examples: testing markers to make sure they write; cutting out the last few "Thought Balloons;" putting chairs in a circle.)*

GET STARTED
1. "Wait" for class to start.
As preteens arrive, adult leaders should be busily finishing their assigned projects. Say: "Oh, I am so sorry. We are just not ready yet. Come on into the room, but please wait over against that wall. It will really help if you just stand quietly in a straight line."

After most preteens have arrived, say: "By the way, be thinking of things you normally do when you are waiting in line. We need to make a list in a few minutes."

As the final part of your "preparation," enlist several preteens to help you attach a large sheet of paper to the wall. Give each person a marker, and direct students to write on the paper some of the things they do while waiting in line.

When preteens have completed the assignment, invite them to be seated in the circle of chairs. Attach Poster 6 to the wall next to the large sheet of paper. Discuss the things preteens might do while waiting.

Give each preteen a "Thought Balloon." Instruct students to write what one of the preteens on the poster might be thinking. Provide tape to attach the balloons to the poster. Discuss responses.

DIG

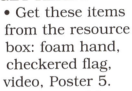

GET READY
• Get these items from the resource box: foam hand, checkered flag, video, Poster 5.
• Gather: Bibles, *Preteen Handbooks*, pencils, markers, seven strips of construction paper, a variety of craft supplies. (See HINT, Step 2.)
• Write one of the following on each of the seven strips of construction paper:
  1. 1 Samuel 16:14-20,23
  2. 1 Samuel 16:21-22
  3. 1 Samuel 17:10-11, 16-22,32-37,48-50
  4. 1 Samuel 17:12-15
  5. 1 Samuel 18:5
  6. 2 Samuel 2:1-4
  7. 2 Samuel 5:1-4
• Enlist an adult leader to share background information from 1 Samuel 16:1-13.
• Secure: VCR and monitor.

GET SET
• Place craft supplies in a central location.
• Push the paper strips into the wrist opening of the foam

STEP 1

HINT
In this step, the more impatient preteens become, the better. Do things to exaggerate their wait. Ask a preteen to hold something for you for a long time. Enlist a volunteer to help you with a task, then keep her waiting for directions or supplies. Wait until the last minute to set up chairs so preteens are left standing. Appear as oblivious to the fact that they are waiting as possible.

STEP 2

HINT
Craft supplies might include poster board, aluminum foil, tape, scissors, construction paper, cotton balls, yarn, glue, paper towel tubes, scraps of cloth, etc.

hand so that only the tips of the paper strips show.
• Set up VCR and monitor. Cue the video to the beginning of the sixth segment, "LifeLine."
• Be sure Poster 5 is attached to the focal wall.

GET STARTED
2. Create props.
Acknowledge the fact that while waiting is almost never easy, it is usually unavoidable. Say: "Waiting two hours to ride a super roller coaster at a theme park is one thing, but imagine waiting many years for a promise to be fulfilled. Today we discover someone in the Bible who did just that. We know a lot about the David, the shepherd boy who became the king of Israel, but we don't usually think about what happened in David's life between those jobs."

Invite seven volunteers to draw a strip of paper from the foam hand. Direct each volunteer to choose one or two other preteens to help him with a project. Give each team these instructions: "Read your assigned Scripture passage. Create a prop to illustrate what was going on in David's life at that time."

Direct attention to the craft supplies you have provided. Tell the teams that they will have five minutes to read the passage and create a prop.

3. Create a time line. After about five minutes, wave the checkered flag as a signal for preteens to return to their seats. Call for volunteers to read aloud the information about David found in "Factionary" on page 29 of

the *Preteen Handbook.*

Choose one boy to be a "statue" of David. Say: "As we look at a time line of David's life, the statue will help us understand what was going on in David's life at that time by using the props you have created."

Invite an adult leader to share background information about David's anointing from 1 Samuel 16:1-13. Remind preteens that several things had to happen before God's promise to make David king was fulfilled.

Call for Team 1 to hand their prop to the "statue" as they explain what happened to David in the Scripture passage they read. When Team 1 completes its report, place the first prop on the floor at the beginning of the time line.

Continue in the same manner with the remaining teams. Add props to the time line as teams make their presentations. Encourage preteens to complete "David's Notebook" on page 30 of their *Preteen Handbooks* while teams present.

4. Review the facts. After all seven teams have reported, thank "David" and invite him to rejoin the group. Guide preteens in a discussion of how each job or experience helped David prepare to serve as king of all Israel.

Ask: "How many times was David anointed before he ruled all of Israel?" *(Three.)* "How old was David when he first became king of Judah?" *(30.)* "How long was it before David became king of all 12 tribes of Israel?" *(Seven years.)*

Emphasize that God

STEP
2

HINT

Be careful that no one is left out as the volunteers choose partners. If you are concerned about the maturity of your preteens in the selection process, assign an adult leader to choose the teams.

Remind adult leaders to float among the teams to answer questions.

helped David wait until it was the proper time for him to become king. God also used the experiences in David's life to prepare him to lead a nation.

5. Watch a video. Introduce the video by explaining that many people have to wait for God's will in their life to be revealed or fulfilled.

Show "LifeLine." Discuss the testimonies of the two people on the video. Allow preteens to share similar stories of people they know or have read about. Ask: "Why is it important that we wait for God to do His will in our lives? (God has the best plan.)

DECIDE

GET READY
• Gather: pencils, *Preteen Handbooks*, white Contact® Paper, scissors, permanent markers, a piece of construction paper.
• Secure: a metronome or something that makes a ticking sound, a toy watch for each preteen.
• Cut strips of white Contact Paper into 4-by-12 inch rectangles to create blank bumper stickers.

GET SET
• Plan to use the key box you created for Session 1. (See page 53, "Get Ready.")
• On a piece of construction paper, write today's memory verse (Psalm 27:14) and place it in the key box.

GET STARTED
6. Discover the key. Call for a volunteer to read the definition of "patience" from the "Factionary" on page 29 of the *Preteen Handbook*. Say: "Long-suffering" is often used as a synonym for 'patience.' Long-suffering is when someone has patience to put up with something for a long time. It involves more than just waiting. Ask: "What did David have to put up with for a long time?" *(Knowing that someday he would be king and yet he still had to do things like tend sheep.)*

Open the "key box" and remove today's memory verse. Lead preteens in reading the verse aloud. Say the memory verse aloud to the rhythm of a metronome. Challenge the preteens to help you create a rhythm that is easily repeated.

7. Create bumper stickers. Instruct preteens to complete "Remember It" on page 29 of the *Preteen Handbook*. Distribute the "bumper stickers." Provide permanent markers. Direct students to create a bumper sticker based on their favorite design from the *Preteen Handbook* activity. When preteens have completed the assignment, call for volunteers to explain their creations. Encourage preteens to place their bumper stickers in an appropriate place to remind them that while they are waiting, God is working.

Close with prayer. Thank God for His plan in our lives. Thank Him for the gift of patience when we must wait for His plan to be fulfilled.

Distribute toy watches as preteens leave. Remind preteens that everything works according to God's timing.

STEP 6

HINT
A metronome is a device musicians use to keep a steady rhythm. It ticks loudly. You can use anything with a steady "tick," or ask the preteens to snap their fingers in time with yours to keep up the rhythm.

STEP 7

HINT
If toy watches are too expensive, consider creating "business cards" by cutting today's memory verse from page 33 of the *Preteen Handbooks*. Attach the verse to a piece of poster board. Add clip art to illustrate the passage of time. (Example: clocks, calendars, etc.)

Stuff to Copy

Make a copy of this article for use in Session 1, Step 5.

Little Wang and Liang

Little Wang, himself a new believer, traveled ten hours with two other Christians to preach to a people group different from his own living in an Asian region with no gospel witness. A village mob met them shouting, "The spirits of the mountains rule our land! You dogs have only been here 500 years and you know nothing. You have stolen our land and now you wish to steal our gods as well. Now you will pay for this!"

Little Wang did pay—with his life. The mob beat the three Christians with sticks and farm tools. Two escaped with broken bones, but an enraged young man beat Little Wang to death. His two brethren limped back home to tell their church and Little Wang's wife and ten-year-old son the sad news.

But church members met and decided the two survivors would go back to preach again. Little Wang's widow, Liang, slowly rose. "I will go too," she said. The church grew silent; everyone knew she might never return.

The trio slipped into the village by night, sleeping fitfully beside a pigpen. When day came, word spread of their presence and another mob quickly formed. But Liang boldly stepped forward and said: "I am the widow of the man you killed. My husband is not dead, however. He is living in paradise with our God. If he were here he would forgive you. I forgive you as well, because God has forgiven me. If you want to hear more about this God, meet us under the big tree outside town this evening."

That night most of the village come to hear about Liang's forgiving God. Many gave their lives to Jesus Christ that night and were discipled in the following days. A few months later three of the new believers visited Liang's church, bringing greetings—and a love offering—from the brand-new church in the once-hostile village. One of them came forward.

"I am the man who murdered Little Wang," he confessed. "The Lord has graciously forgiven me and I ask your forgiveness as well. I, and our entire church, owe an eternal debt of gratitude to Little Wang and Liang for bringing us the message of life. We want to give this offering to help support Liang and we wish to pledge monthly support."

Little Wang wasn't the only martyr of 1998, Liang wasn't the only Christian widow. Their courage and obedience typify the faith lived by millions of Baptists and Great Commission partners working worldwide with more than 4,500 International Mission Board missionaries.

Reprinted from Baptist Press *(February 18, 1999). Used by permission.*

Thought Balloon

Enlarge, make copies, and cut out for use in Session 3, Step 1. Each preteen present will need one.

Person Outline

Enlarge and make a copy for each preteen for use in Session 2, Step 1.

Bonus Session

A Savior Is Born

How This Session Relates to Salvation

Could you trust a Savior who neither understood nor felt compassion for the people He came to save? Jesus is not a cold, impersonal deliverer. Through human birth, Jesus became "one of us." He is a Savior who understands our needs.

FOCAL PASSAGES:
Luke 1:26-35; 2:1-20

MEMORY VERSE:
I bring you good news of great joy that will be for all the people. Today in the town of David a Savior has been born to you; he is Christ the Lord." Luke 2:10b-11

LIFE DESTINATION:
Preteens will celebrate the birth of Christ as they realize the significance of His miraculous birth.

Bible Study for Leaders

Pause for a moment and name the people God chose to bring about the coming of His Son: a carpenter, a Jewish girl, anonymous shepherds. As we think about the miracle of Christ's birth, we marvel at God's use of ordinary people to accomplish His extraordinary purpose.

The Announcement

Even Nazareth, the place where the story begins, had a "nobody" reputation. Nazarenes were considered to be uncultured, uneducated, and unbelieving. Still, two of its residents were chosen to parent the Messiah. Young Mary certainly didn't expect a visit from Gabriel, God's message bearer. She certainly didn't expect the message to be that she would give birth to the Son of God. Gabriel described the mission of her baby: He would be the Savior, and would fulfill God's promise to bring a Messiah to the world through the family line of David.

Mary was legally pledged to be married to Joseph, and was troubled about the practical implications of her pregnancy. Gabriel reassured Mary that the circumstances were under God's control, and she willingly undertook her assignment.

The Arrival

The Savior was to be born in Bethlehem (Micah 5:2). So how did God move an unmarried couple over 80 miles south—

a huge journey in those days—to carry out the prophecy? He simply arranged history to suit His purposes! A Roman census was declared, probably to identify all the taxable Jewish families in Palestine. Joseph chose not to leave his embarrassingly pregnant fiancee in Nazareth; he brought her with him to the town of his ancestors.

Unfortunately, other travelers arrived at the inn before Mary and Joseph. The inn was most likely a walled-in courtyard with a well. Crowded out of even those semi-private accommodations, Mary probably endured labor and delivery in an uncomfortable stable or cave.

Amazing!

And who were the first guests to greet the Savior? They were shepherds, snubbed by other Jews because their outdoor lifestyle did not allow them to observe the washings and rituals required by ceremonial law. Camping out with their animals, the shepherds were awestruck when an angel appeared with the good news that Christ, the Messiah, had been born nearby.

The shepherds did not seem to recognize the glorious irony that the Messiah would be snugly wrapped in cloths, napping in a feed box. Instead, they hurried into town to see Him for themselves. Giddy with joy, the shepherds told everyone they met that they had personally met their Savior—no ordinary baby!

DISCUSS AND DO

GET READY

• Gather: a variety of secular Christmas decorations such as tree lights; plastic snowmen and Santas; Christmas stockings; cartoon character ornaments; mistletoe; a "pin-the-tail-on-the-reindeer" game.
• Encourage adult workers to wear Santa hats and secular Christmas shirts and accessories.
• Secure: a CD or tape player and recordings of secular Christmas carols, table.
• Prepare Christmas refreshments for your class.
• Plan a simple party game with a secular Christmas theme.

GET SET

• Decorate your department with secular Christmas items.
• Set up the CD or tape player and recording.
• Arrange the refreshments on the table.

GET STARTED

1. Enjoy a tacky Christmas party. Play the recordings you brought and "pull out all the stops" as you merrily welcome preteens to your Christmas session. Serve refreshments, play games, and listen to "Santa" music. Register no sign that your party is highly out of place in a Bible study setting. Participate in the secular celebration for about a quarter of the session.

2. Discover what's missing. Stop the music and invite preteens to be seated. Say:

"We've had fun this morning, but something seems to be missing from our Christmas celebration. What is it?" (*So far there has been no mention of Jesus' birth.*) Point to several of the decorations and ask: "Does (a jolly snowman) reflect Jesus' birth in any way? How about these (elf ears)?" Discuss.

Encourage preteens to name Christmas traditions that in no way recognize the birth of Christ. Say: "We are not going to forget what Christmas is really all about! Let's spend the rest of our session truly celebrating the arrival of God's Son."

DIG

GET READY

• Gather: Bibles, pencils, *Preteen Handbooks.*

GET STARTED

3. Reveal what preteens really know about Christmas. Say: "No doubt you've heard the Christmas story dozens of times. You can show off your Christmas knowledge by scoring well on this little aptitude test." Distribute *Preteen Handbooks* and challenge students to complete the "Christmas IQ Test" on page 32. Share answers and congratulate students with a 70 percent or better score. (*Answers: 1. Nazareth—Luke 2:4; 2. False—Luke 2:5; 3. d; 4. No innkeeper is mentioned in Luke 2; 5. Luke 2 does not specifically describe Jesus' birthplace; 6. Luke 2 does not mention animals; 7. False—Luke 2:12,15-16; 8. Unknown—Matthew 2:1;*

9. In a house—Matthew 2:11; 10. False—Matthew and Luke.)

Call for volunteers to name legends or traditions that are associated with the Christmas story that are not mentioned in the Bible. (*Examples: animals talked at midnight when Jesus was born, little drummer boy, three wise men, wise men were present at Jesus' birth, etc.*)

Say: "Even one incorrect answer on the IQ test may indicate that we need to examine the story of Jesus' birth a little more carefully."

4. Listen to the Christmas story. Form two listening teams. Instruct Team 1 to be ready to identify the ordinary people God involved in His Son's birth. Instruct Team 2 to identify the extraordinary things God did to and through those people.

Open your Bible and read Luke 1:26-38, 2:1-20 as preteens listen. Call on each team to report.

5. Focus on Jesus' characteristics. Say: "Even Jesus' name was extraordinary. Jesus means 'anointed one' or 'Yahweh is salvation.' The Bible gives Jesus other names that help us realize what a special person God sent into the world."

Direct preteens to form small groups and complete "No Ordinary Baby" on page 31 of the *Preteen Handbook*. (*Answers: John 14:6—Way, Truth, Life; John 10:11—Good Shepherd; John 1:7—Light; Isaiah 7:14—Immanuel; Isaiah 9:6—Wonderful Counselor, Mighty God, Everlasting Father, Prince of Peace.*)

Encourage each group to select one name from the Bible verses they examined and explain how it relates to Jesus' personality.

DECIDE
GET READY
• Get these items from the resource box: foam hand, key, checkered flag.
• Gather: *Preteen Handbooks*, pencils, poster board, markers, construction paper, tape, a large candle.
• Collect a variety of Christian Christmas decorations and symbols (nativity set minus the wise men; ornaments shaped like lambs, doves, crosses; etc.)
• Secure: a cassette or CD player, a recording of instrumental Christmas hymns.

GET SET
• Set up the cassette or CD player. Cue the recording to the song(s) you selected.

GET STARTED
6. Decide to celebrate Jesus this season. Say: "Think about the ways you and your family celebrate Christmas. Does your family have some traditions that truly honor Jesus' birth?" Invite volunteers to share their family traditions. Challenge preteens to create at least one new tradition for their family this year that focuses completely on Jesus. Guide preteens to complete "Celebration Creation" on page 32 of the *Preteen Handbook*. Invite volunteers to share their most creative ideas.

STEP 6

Hint
Be prepared to share special things you and your family do to honor Jesus' birth. Remind preteens that giving gifts out of love, ministering to those in need, and worshiping God are ways to honor Christ's birth.

STEP 7

HINT

Consider bringing a camera for a class photograph. Take a picture of the entire group posing under the Christ-centered decorations they created. (If possible, mail a finished print to each student before Christmas instead of a Christmas card.)

7. Transform your room. Sweep your hand toward the secular decorations and say: "Now these decorations seem really out of place! Let's redecorate!"

Play the instrumental recording you brought as you lead teams of students to:

• remove all secular decorations.

• create banners or posters that illustrate the names of Jesus. (Refer students to the "No Ordinary Baby" activity in the *Preteen Handbook*.) Encourage students to use one or more of the gadgets from the resource box.

• set out the Christian Christmas decorations you brought.

Adult leaders can exchange secular shirts and accessories for shirts and accessories with a Christian emphasis. *(Examples: items featuring "Jesus is the reason for the season," angels, Bible verses.)*

8. Experience the Christmas story. After redecorating your room, invite preteens to be seated on the floor in the middle of the room. Turn off the lights and darken the room as much as possible. Light the large candle. Encourage preteens to sit quietly and listen carefully as you read aloud Luke 1:26-38; 2:1-20 again.

Challenge preteens to put themselves in Joseph's place. Ask: "How do you think Joseph felt when he found out that Mary was going to have a baby?" Read the account of Jesus' birth from Matthew 1:18-25. Ask: "How do you think Joseph felt when he could not find a place for them to stay in Bethlehem?"

Next, challenge preteens to put themselves in Mary's place. Ask: "How do you think Mary felt when the angel told her she was going to have a child? How do you think she felt when she found out she was going to have to travel a long distance close to the time her baby was due? Do you think it was scary for Mary to have her baby in a strange place in a strange town? Why or why not?"

Invite preteens to put themselves in the shepherds' place. Ask: "What would you have done if you had been in that field when the angels appeared?"

Remind preteens that Mary, Joseph, and the shepherds were ordinary people whom God used in extraordinary ways.

Say: "God wants to use each of us in a special way." Ask: "What are some ways God can use us during this Christmas season to accomplish His purpose?" Discuss.

9. Celebrate Jesus with prayer. Lead preteens to stand in a circle facing outward. Encourage students to think of gifts they can give to God to honor Christ's birth. As you play a quiet Christmas carol, guide preteens to pray silently with their eyes open, thanking God for Jesus' miraculous birth. Dismiss with your wishes for a merry and meaningful Christmas.